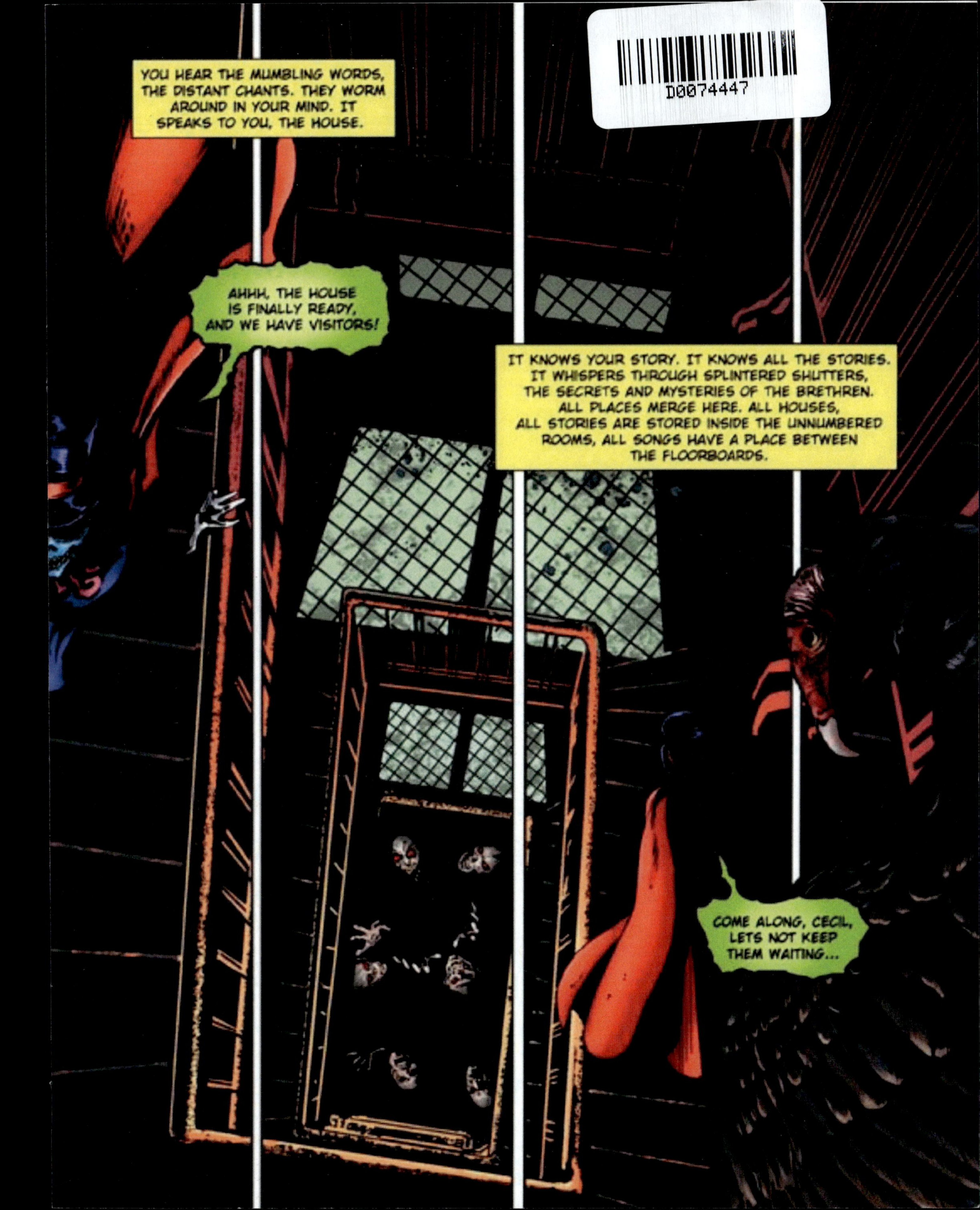
YOU HEAR THE MUMBLING WORDS, THE DISTANT CHANTS. THEY WORM AROUND IN YOUR MIND. IT SPEAKS TO YOU, THE HOUSE.
AHHH, THE HOUSE IS FINALLY READY, AND WE HAVE VISITORS!
IT KNOWS YOUR STORY. IT KNOWS ALL THE STORIES. IT WHISPERS THROUGH SPLINTERED SHUTTERS, THE SECRETS AND MYSTERIES OF THE BRETHREN. ALL PLACES MERGE HERE. ALL HOUSES, ALL STORIES ARE STORED INSIDE THE UNNUMBERED ROOMS, ALL SONGS HAVE A PLACE BETWEEN THE FLOORBOARDS.
COME ALONG, CECIL, LETS NOT KEEP THEM WAITING...

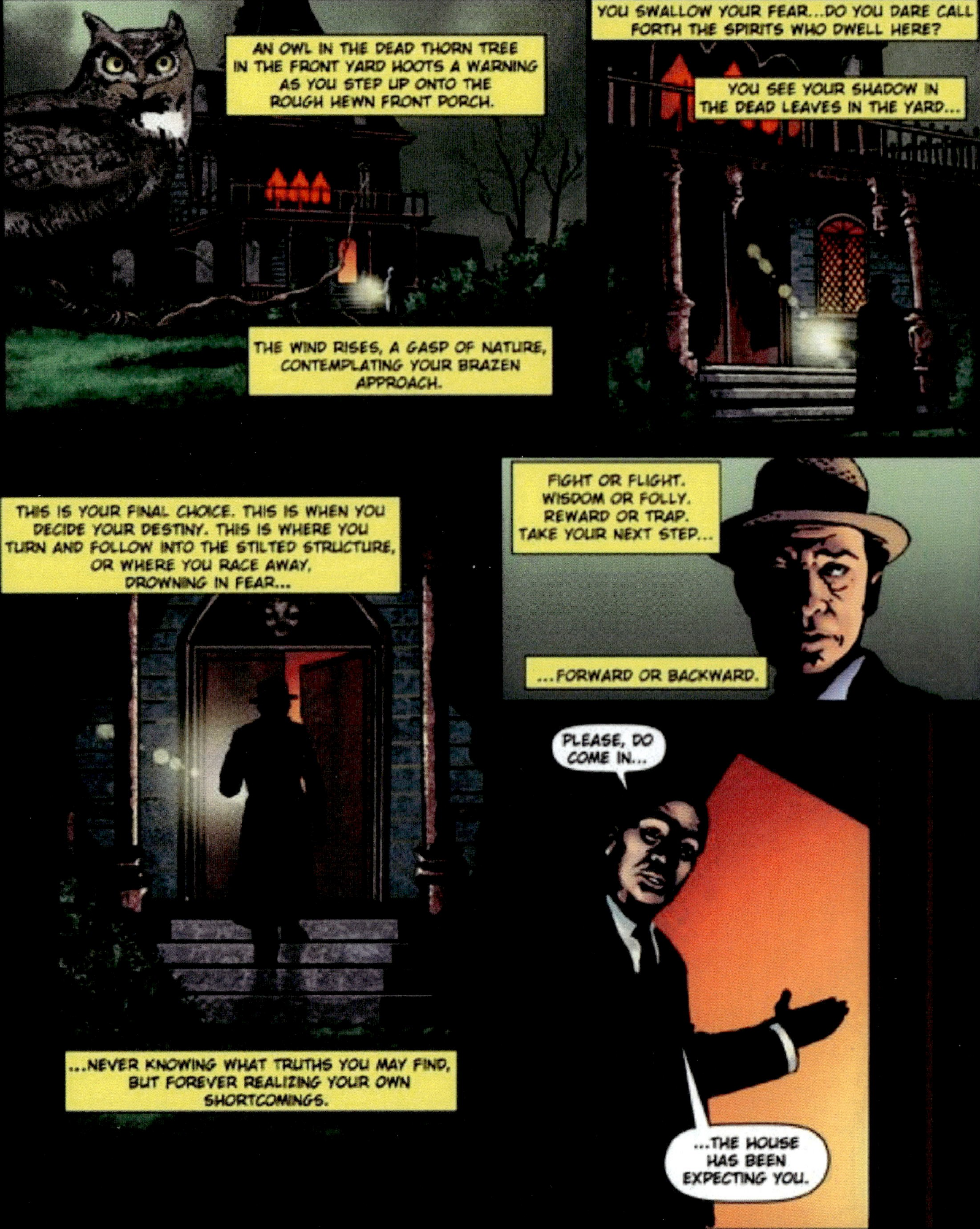
AN OWL IN THE DEAD THORN TREE IN THE FRONT YARD HOOTS A WARNING AS YOU STEP UP ONTO THE ROUGH HEWN FRONT PORCH.
THE WIND RISES, A GASP OF NATURE, CONTEMPLATING YOUR BRAZEN APPROACH.
YOU SWALLOW YOUR FEAR...DO YOU DARE CALL FORTH THE SPIRITS WHO DWELL HERE?
YOU SEE YOUR SHADOW IN THE DEAD LEAVES IN THE YARD...
THIS IS YOUR FINAL CHOICE. THIS IS WHEN YOU DECIDE YOUR DESTINY. THIS IS WHERE YOU TURN AND FOLLOW INTO THE STILTED STRUCTURE, OR WHERE YOU RACE AWAY, DROWNING IN FEAR...
...NEVER KNOWING WHAT TRUTHS YOU MAY FIND, BUT FOREVER REALIZING YOUR OWN SHORTCOMINGS.
FIGHT OR FLIGHT. WISDOM OR FOLLY. REWARD OR TRAP. TAKE YOUR NEXT STEP...
...FORWARD OR BACKWARD.
PLEASE, DO COME IN...
...THE HOUSE HAS BEEN EXPECTING YOU.

HERE ARE NIGHTS LIKE THIS AT THE HOUSE OF SPADES NEXUS, WHERE THE HUNGER FOR THE POWER GAME BECOMES INSATIABLE.

THE POND, THE CEMETERY, AND THE HOUSE VIE FOR DOMINANCE AND MYSTICAL ADVANTAGE, BETWEEN THE TRINITY.

THEY SAY THE HOUSE ALWAYS WINS, AND THAT MAY BE TRUE...

BUT SOMETIMES, IT ONLY WINS BECAUSE IT KNOWS WHEN TO RETREAT.

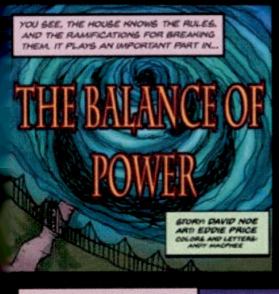

YOU SEE, THE HOUSE KNOWS THE RULES, AND THE RAMIFICATIONS FOR BREAKING THEM. IT PLAYS AN IMPORTANT PART IN...

THE BALANCE OF POWER

STORY: DAVID NOE
ART: EDDIE PRICE
COLORS AND LETTERS: ANDY MACPHEE

AFTER THE WINTER, THE GROWING SEASON URGES THE POND TO COME OUT OF THE DEEP FREEZE, WITH A PALATE TO CONQUER.

THE POND RAKES ACROSS TOWARDS THE CEMETERY, IN AN EFFORT TO ABSORB AND CONTROL ANY ESSENCE IT TOUCHES.

BUT THE CEMETERY HAS IT'S OWN BORDERS AND GUARDIANS, THAT STAND AT THE READY TO PLAY THE AGE-OLD GAME.

IT HAS CALLED THEM TO THIS SPOT, WITH THE PROMISE OF POWER!

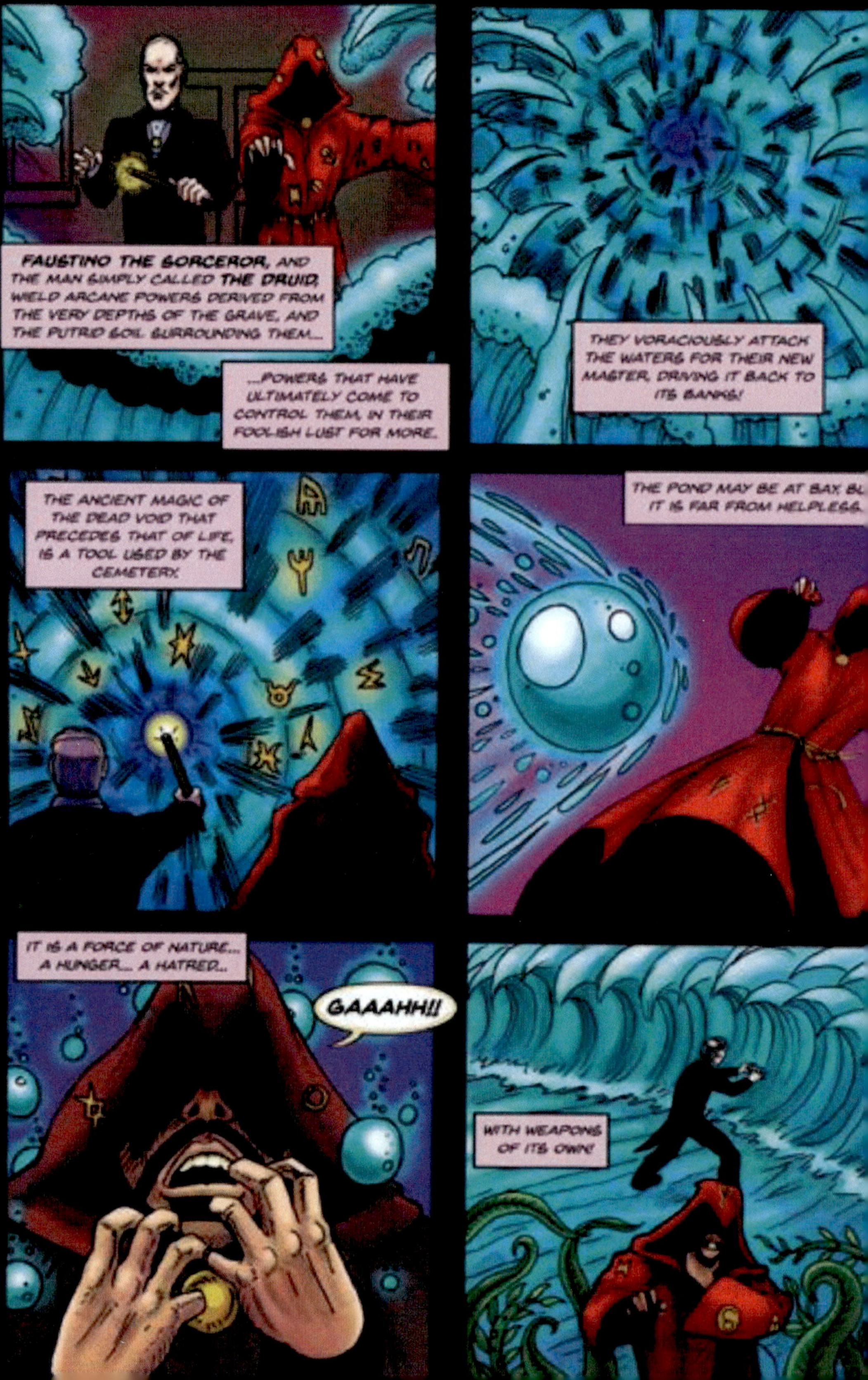
FAUSTINO THE SORCEROR, AND THE MAN SIMPLY CALLED THE DRUID, WIELD ARCANE POWERS DERIVED FROM THE VERY DEPTHS OF THE GRAVE, AND THE PUTRID SOIL SURROUNDING THEM...
...POWERS THAT HAVE ULTIMATELY COME TO CONTROL THEM, IN THEIR FOOLISH LUST FOR MORE.
THEY VORACIOUSLY ATTACK THE WATERS FOR THEIR NEW MASTER, DRIVING IT BACK TO ITS BANKS!
THE ANCIENT MAGIC OF THE DEAD VOID THAT PRECEDES THAT OF LIFE, IS A TOOL USED BY THE CEMETERY.
THE POND MAY BE AT BAY, BU IT IS FAR FROM HELPLESS.
IT IS A FORCE OF NATURE... A HUNGER... A HATRED...
GAAAHH!!
WITH WEAPONS OF ITS OWN!

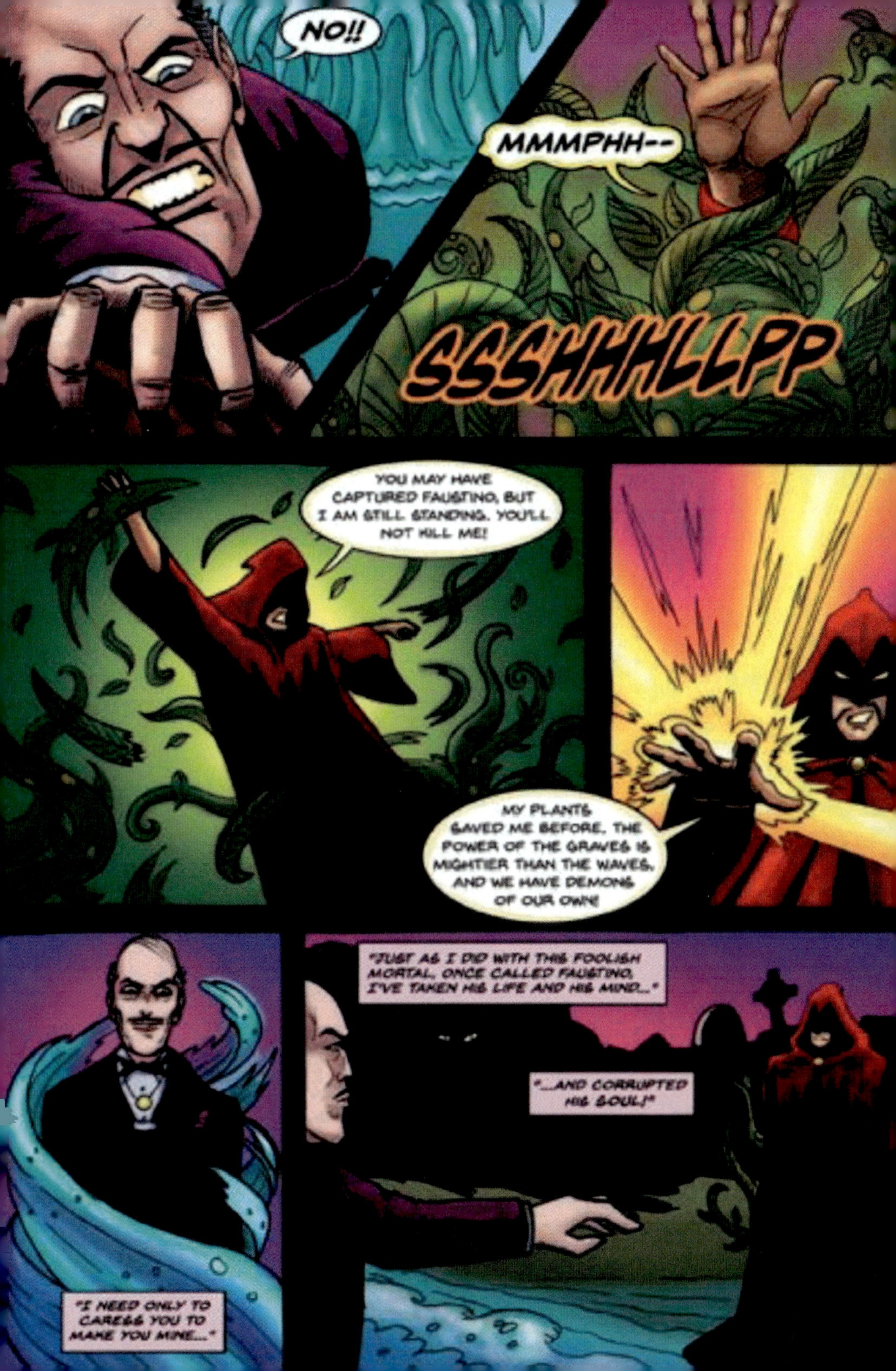
NO!!
MMMPHH--
SSSHHHLLPP
YOU MAY HAVE CAPTURED FAUSTINO, BUT I AM STILL STANDING. YOU'LL NOT KILL ME!
MY PLANTS SAVED ME BEFORE. THE POWER OF THE GRAVES IS MIGHTIER THAN THE WAVES, AND WE HAVE DEMONS OF OUR OWN!
"I NEED ONLY TO CARESS YOU TO MAKE YOU MINE..."
"JUST AS I DID WITH THIS FOOLISH MORTAL, ONCE CALLED FAUSTINO, I'VE TAKEN HIS LIFE AND HIS MIND..."
"...AND CORRUPTED HIS SOUL!"

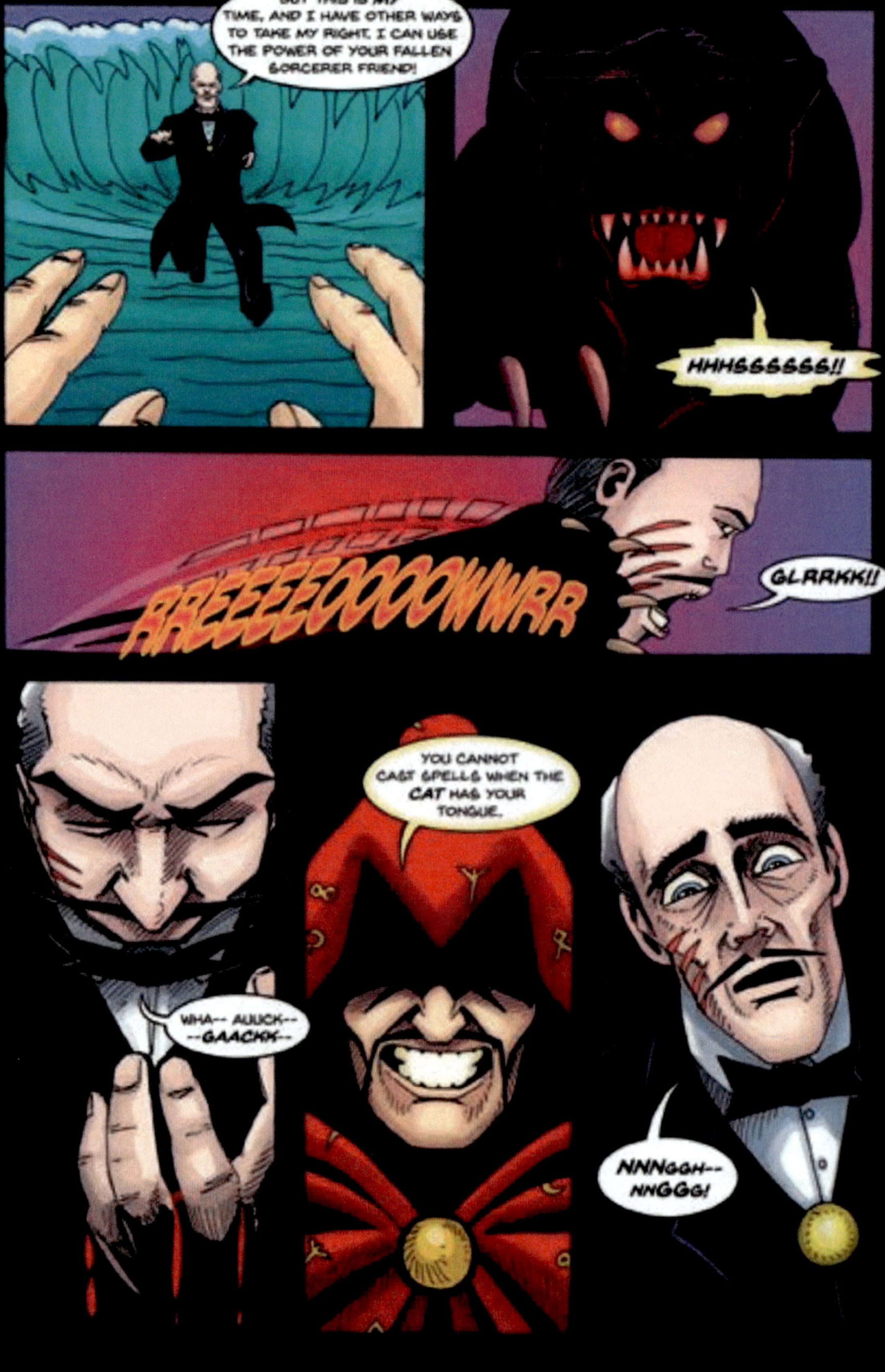
BUT THIS IS MY TIME, AND I HAVE OTHER WAYS TO TAKE MY RIGHT. I CAN USE THE POWER OF YOUR FALLEN SORCERER FRIEND!
HHHSSSSSSS!!
RREEEEOOOOWWRR
GLRRKK!!
YOU CANNOT CAST SPELLS WHEN THE CAT HAS YOUR TONGUE.
WHA-- AUUCK-- --GAACKK--
NNNGGH-- NNGGG!

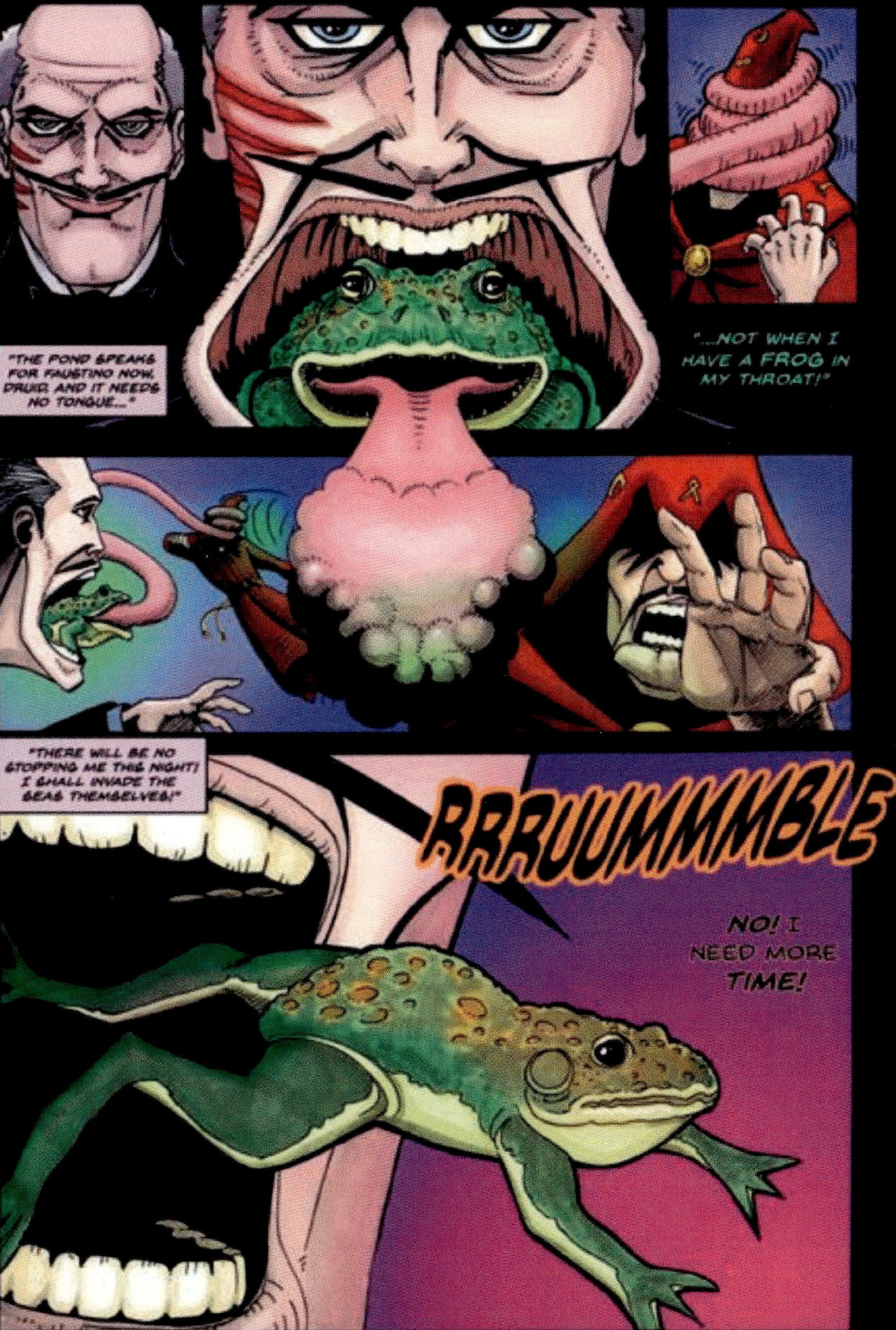
"THE POND SPEAKS FOR FAUSTINO NOW, DRUID, AND IT NEEDS NO TONGUE..."
"...NOT WHEN I HAVE A FROG IN MY THROAT!"
"THERE WILL BE NO STOPPING ME THIS NIGHT! I SHALL INVADE THE SEAS THEMSELVES!"
RRRUUMMMBLE
NO! I NEED MORE TIME!

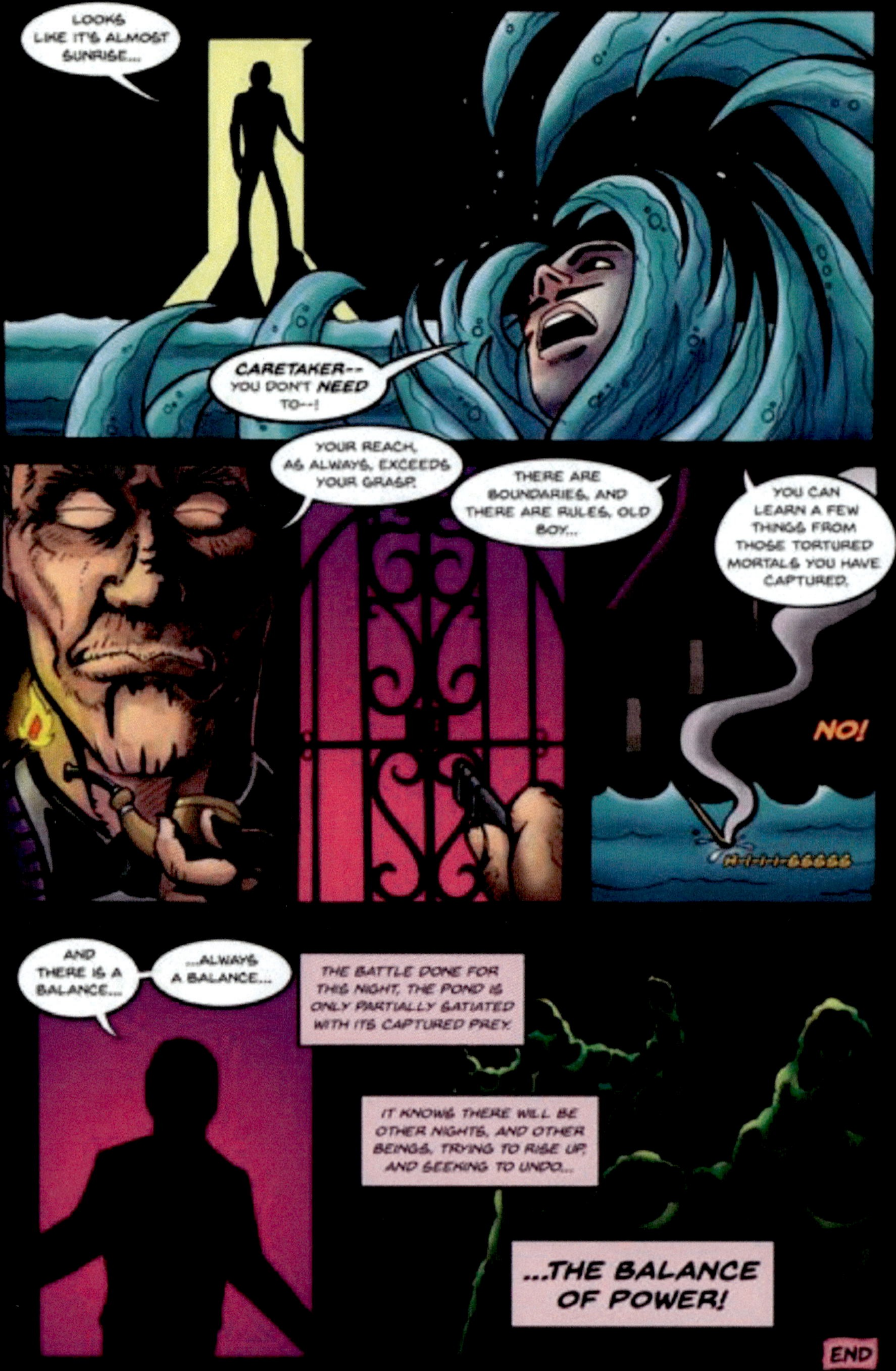

LOOKS LIKE IT'S ALMOST SUNRISE...
CARETAKER-- YOU DON'T NEED TO--!
YOUR REACH, AS ALWAYS, EXCEEDS YOUR GRASP.
THERE ARE BOUNDARIES, AND THERE ARE RULES, OLD BOY...
YOU CAN LEARN A FEW THINGS FROM THOSE TORTURED MORTALS YOU HAVE CAPTURED.
NO!
N-I-I-I-GGGGG
AND THERE IS A BALANCE...
...ALWAYS A BALANCE...
THE BATTLE DONE FOR THIS NIGHT, THE POND IS ONLY PARTIALLY SATIATED WITH ITS CAPTURED PREY.
IT KNOWS THERE WILL BE OTHER NIGHTS, AND OTHER BEINGS, TRYING TO RISE UP, AND SEEKING TO UNDO...
...THE BALANCE OF POWER!
END

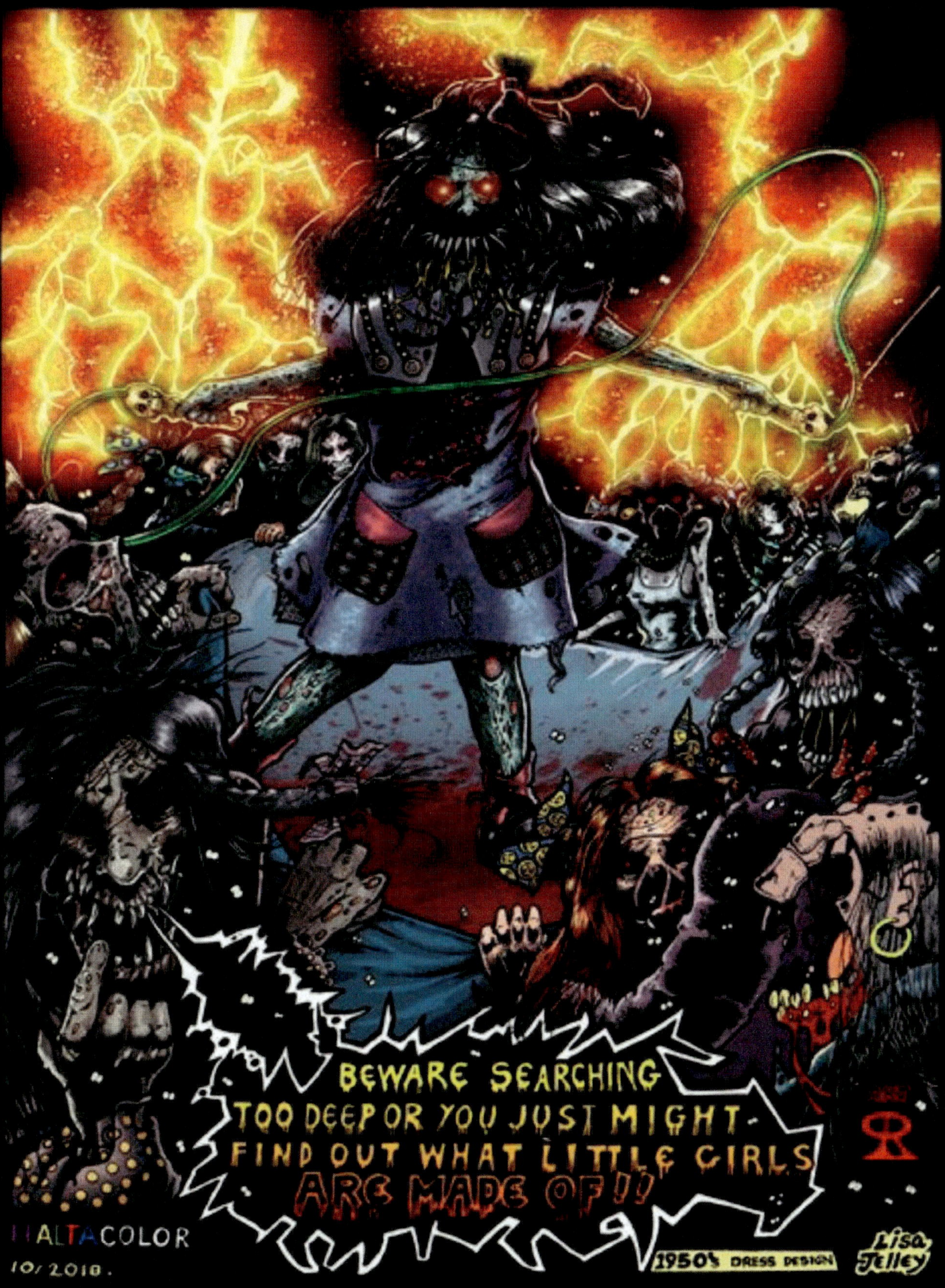
BEWARE SEARCHING TOO DEEP OR YOU JUST MIGHT FIND OUT WHAT LITTLE GIRLS ARE MADE OF !!
1950's DRESS DESIGN
Lisa Jelley
ALTACOLOR
10/2018.

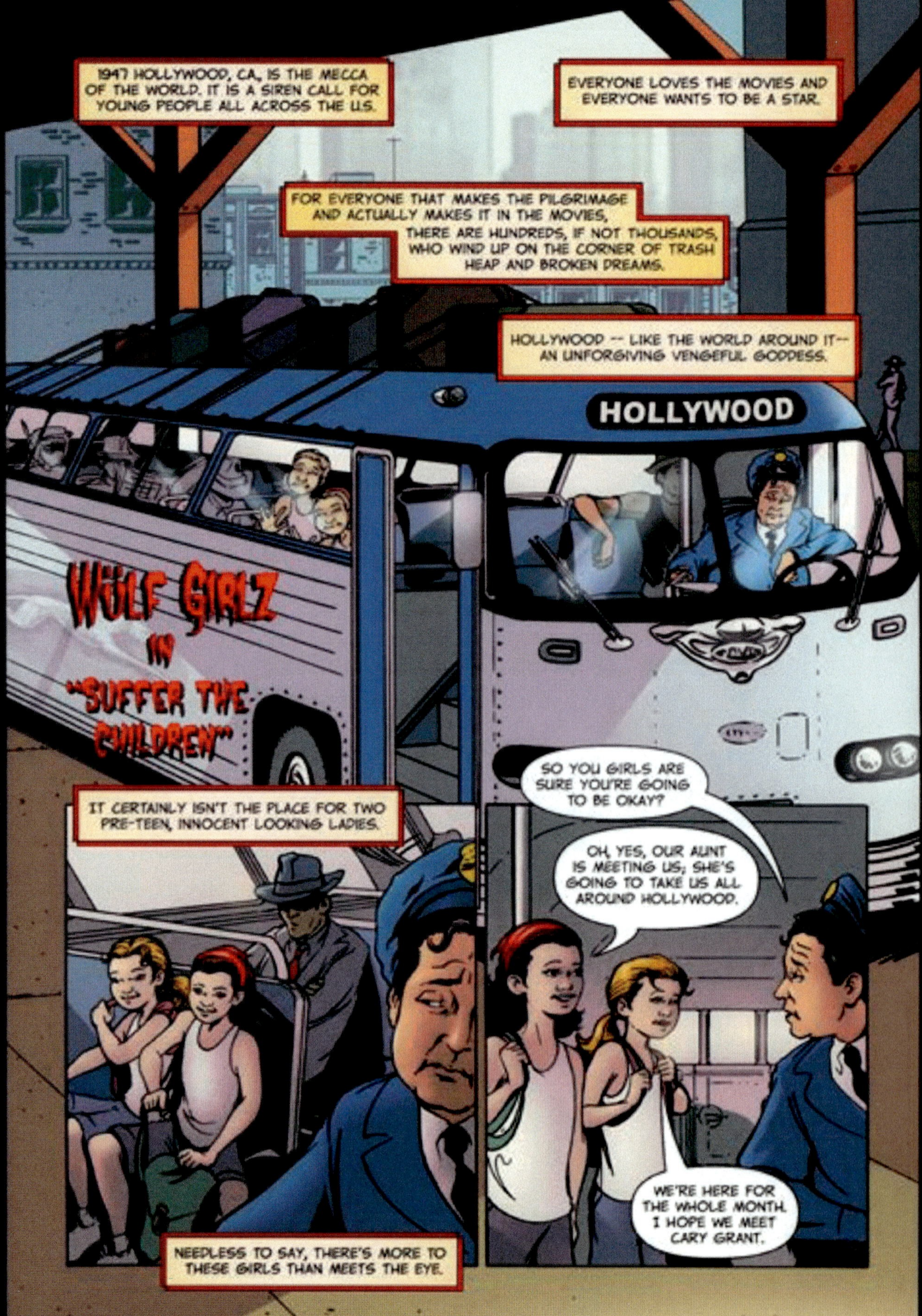
1947 HOLLYWOOD, CA., IS THE MECCA OF THE WORLD. IT IS A SIREN CALL FOR YOUNG PEOPLE ALL ACROSS THE U.S.
EVERYONE LOVES THE MOVIES AND EVERYONE WANTS TO BE A STAR.
FOR EVERYONE THAT MAKES THE PILGRIMAGE AND ACTUALLY MAKES IT IN THE MOVIES,
THERE ARE HUNDREDS, IF NOT THOUSANDS, WHO WIND UP ON THE CORNER OF TRASH HEAP AND BROKEN DREAMS.
HOLLYWOOD -- LIKE THE WORLD AROUND IT-- AN UNFORGIVING VENGEFUL GODDESS.
HOLLYWOOD
WÜLF GIRLZ
IN
"SUFFER THE CHILDREN"
IT CERTAINLY ISN'T THE PLACE FOR TWO PRE-TEEN, INNOCENT LOOKING LADIES.
SO YOU GIRLS ARE SURE YOU'RE GOING TO BE OKAY?
OH, YES, OUR AUNT IS MEETING US; SHE'S GOING TO TAKE US ALL AROUND HOLLYWOOD.
WE'RE HERE FOR THE WHOLE MONTH. I HOPE WE MEET CARY GRANT.
NEEDLESS TO SAY, THERE'S MORE TO THESE GIRLS THAN MEETS THE EYE.

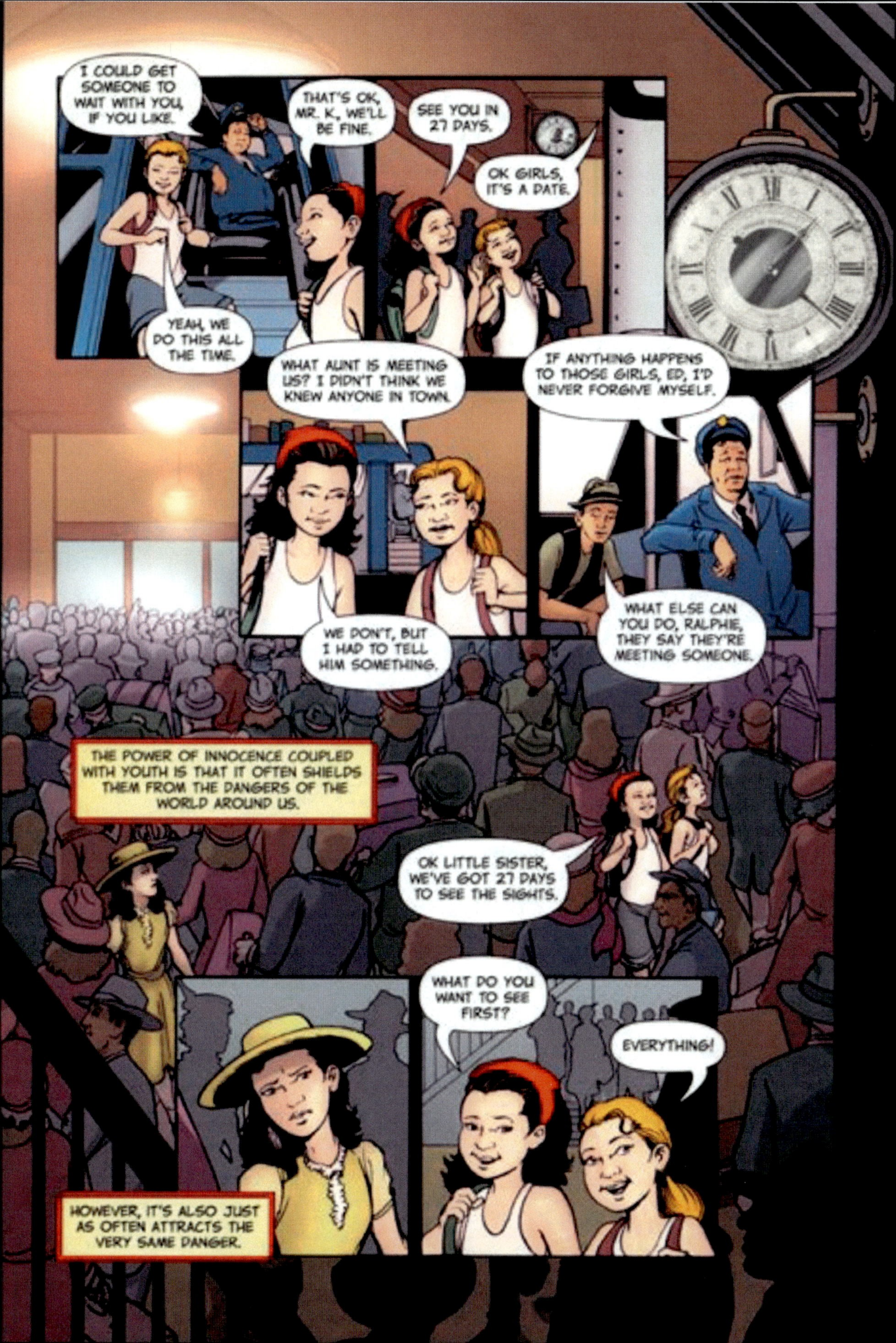

I COULD GET SOMEONE TO WAIT WITH YOU, IF YOU LIKE.
YEAH, WE DO THIS ALL THE TIME.
THAT'S OK, MR. K., WE'LL BE FINE.
SEE YOU IN 27 DAYS.
OK GIRLS, IT'S A DATE.
WHAT AUNT IS MEETING US? I DIDN'T THINK WE KNEW ANYONE IN TOWN.
WE DON'T, BUT I HAD TO TELL HIM SOMETHING.
IF ANYTHING HAPPENS TO THOSE GIRLS, ED, I'D NEVER FORGIVE MYSELF.
WHAT ELSE CAN YOU DO, RALPHIE, THEY SAY THEY'RE MEETING SOMEONE.
THE POWER OF INNOCENCE COUPLED WITH YOUTH IS THAT IT OFTEN SHIELDS THEM FROM THE DANGERS OF THE WORLD AROUND US.
OK LITTLE SISTER, WE'VE GOT 27 DAYS TO SEE THE SIGHTS.
HOWEVER, IT'S ALSO JUST AS OFTEN ATTRACTS THE VERY SAME DANGER.
WHAT DO YOU WANT TO SEE FIRST?
EVERYTHING!

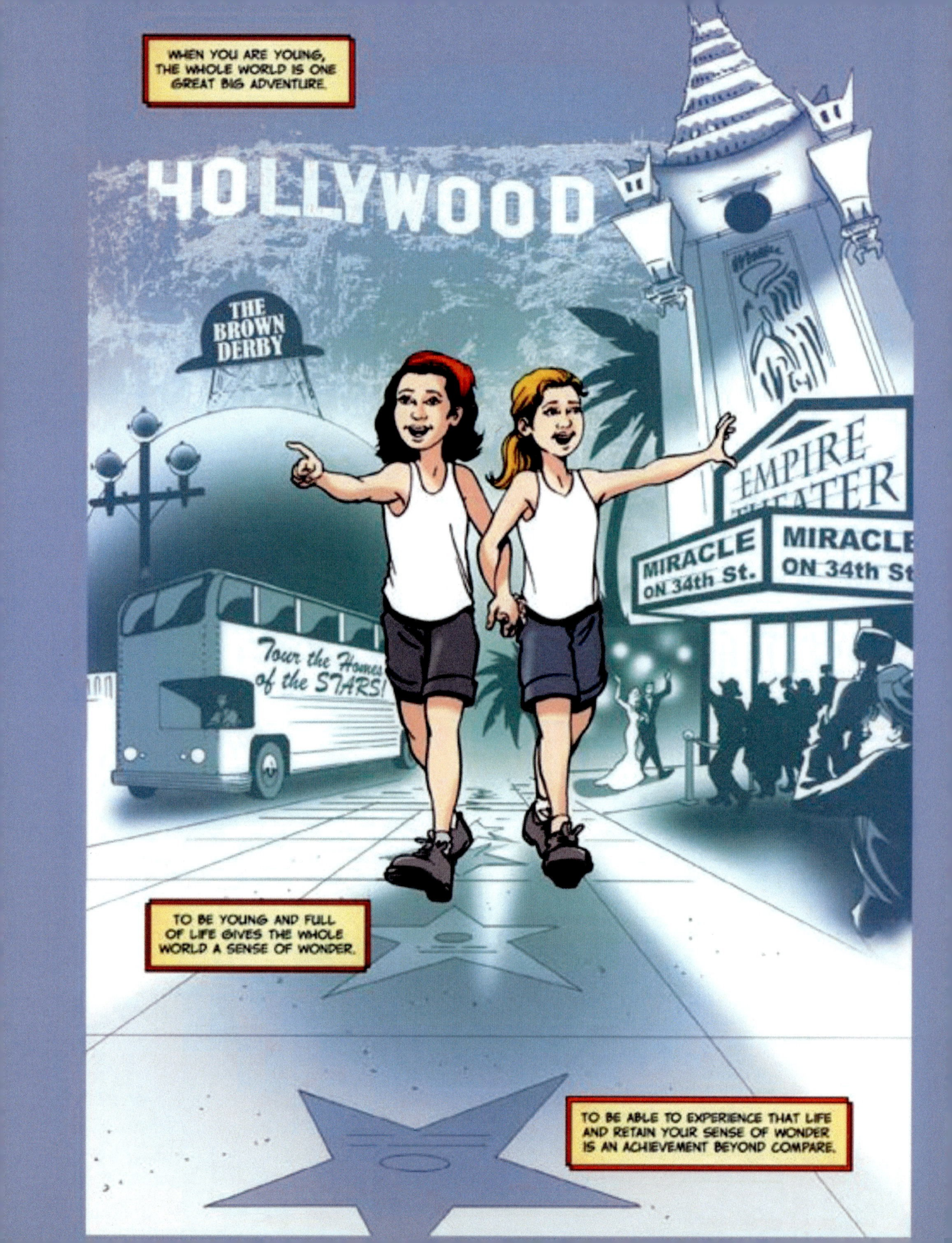
WHEN YOU ARE YOUNG, THE WHOLE WORLD IS ONE GREAT BIG ADVENTURE.
HOLLYWOOD
THE BROWN DERBY
Tour the Homes of the STARS!
EMPIRE THEATER
MIRACLE ON 34th St.
MIRACLE ON 34th St
TO BE YOUNG AND FULL OF LIFE GIVES THE WHOLE WORLD A SENSE OF WONDER.
TO BE ABLE TO EXPERIENCE THAT LIFE AND RETAIN YOUR SENSE OF WONDER IS AN ACHIEVEMENT BEYOND COMPARE.

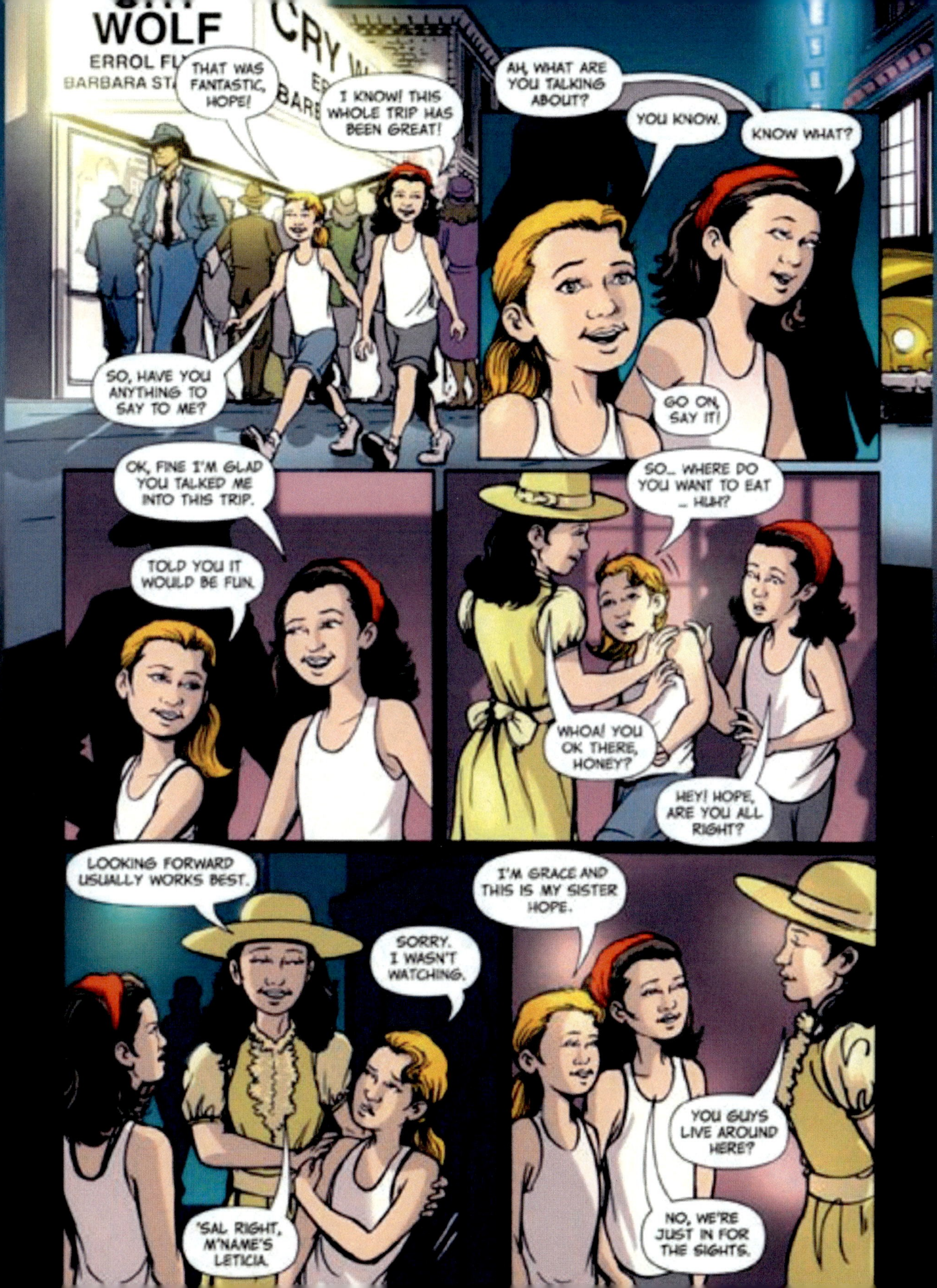
WOLF
ERROL FL
BARBARA STA
CRY W
THAT WAS FANTASTIC, HOPE!
I KNOW! THIS WHOLE TRIP HAS BEEN GREAT!
SO, HAVE YOU ANYTHING TO SAY TO ME?
AH, WHAT ARE YOU TALKING ABOUT?
YOU KNOW.
KNOW WHAT?
GO ON, SAY IT!
OK, FINE I'M GLAD YOU TALKED ME INTO THIS TRIP.
TOLD YOU IT WOULD BE FUN.
SO... WHERE DO YOU WANT TO EAT ... HUH?
WHOA! YOU OK THERE, HONEY?
HEY! HOPE, ARE YOU ALL RIGHT?
LOOKING FORWARD USUALLY WORKS BEST.
SORRY. I WASN'T WATCHING.
'SAL RIGHT, M'NAME'S LETICIA.
I'M GRACE AND THIS IS MY SISTER HOPE.
YOU GUYS LIVE AROUND HERE?
NO, WE'RE JUST IN FOR THE SIGHTS.

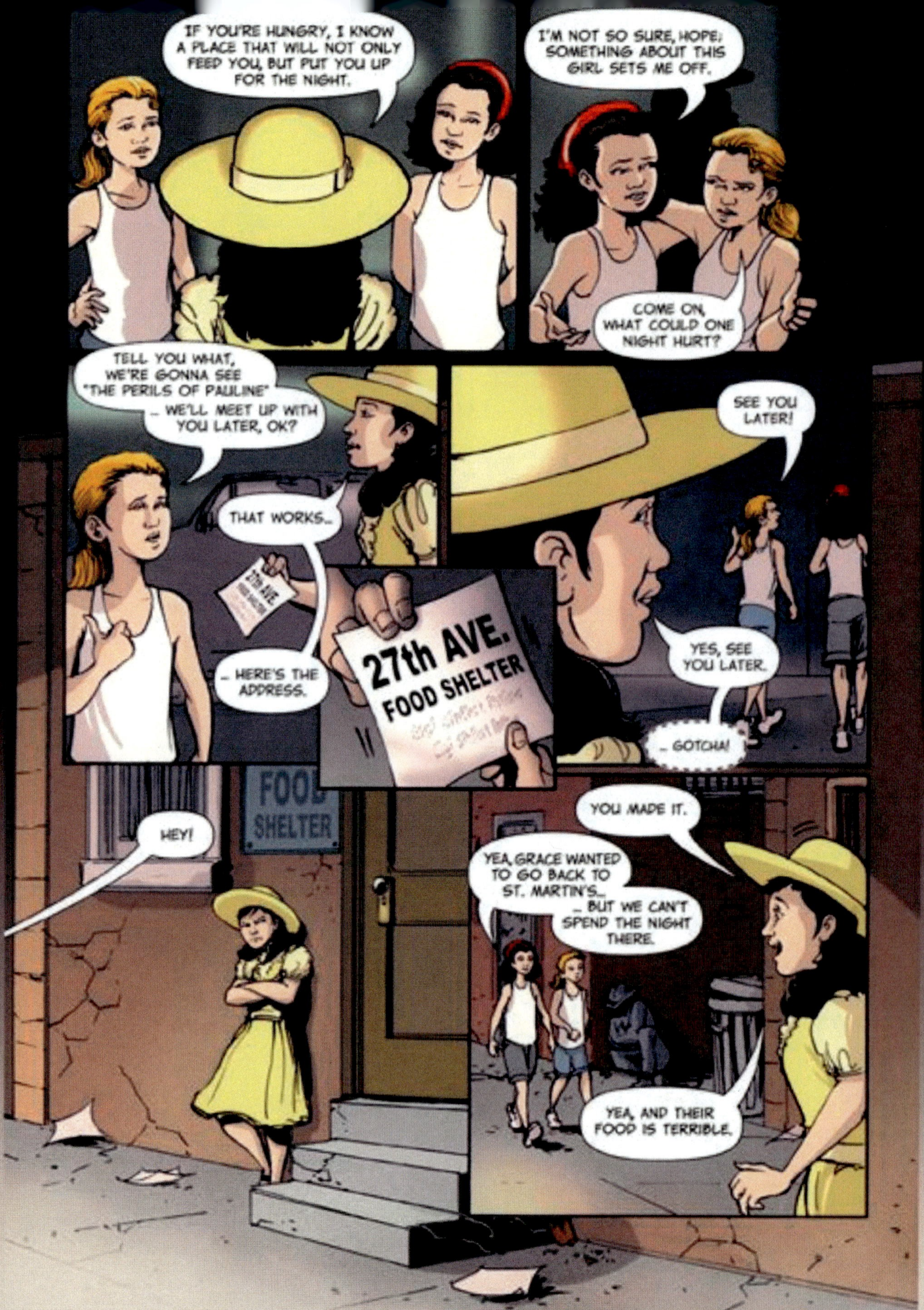
IF YOU'RE HUNGRY, I KNOW A PLACE THAT WILL NOT ONLY FEED YOU, BUT PUT YOU UP FOR THE NIGHT.
I'M NOT SO SURE, HOPE; SOMETHING ABOUT THIS GIRL SETS ME OFF.
COME ON, WHAT COULD ONE NIGHT HURT?
TELL YOU WHAT, WE'RE GONNA SEE "THE PERILS OF PAULINE"
... WE'LL MEET UP WITH YOU LATER, OK?
THAT WORKS...
... HERE'S THE ADDRESS.
27th AVE.
FOOD SHELTER
SEE YOU LATER!
YES, SEE YOU LATER.
... GOTCHA!
FOOD SHELTER
HEY!
YOU MADE IT.
YEA, GRACE WANTED TO GO BACK TO ST. MARTIN'S...
... BUT WE CAN'T SPEND THE NIGHT THERE.
YEA, AND THEIR FOOD IS TERRIBLE.

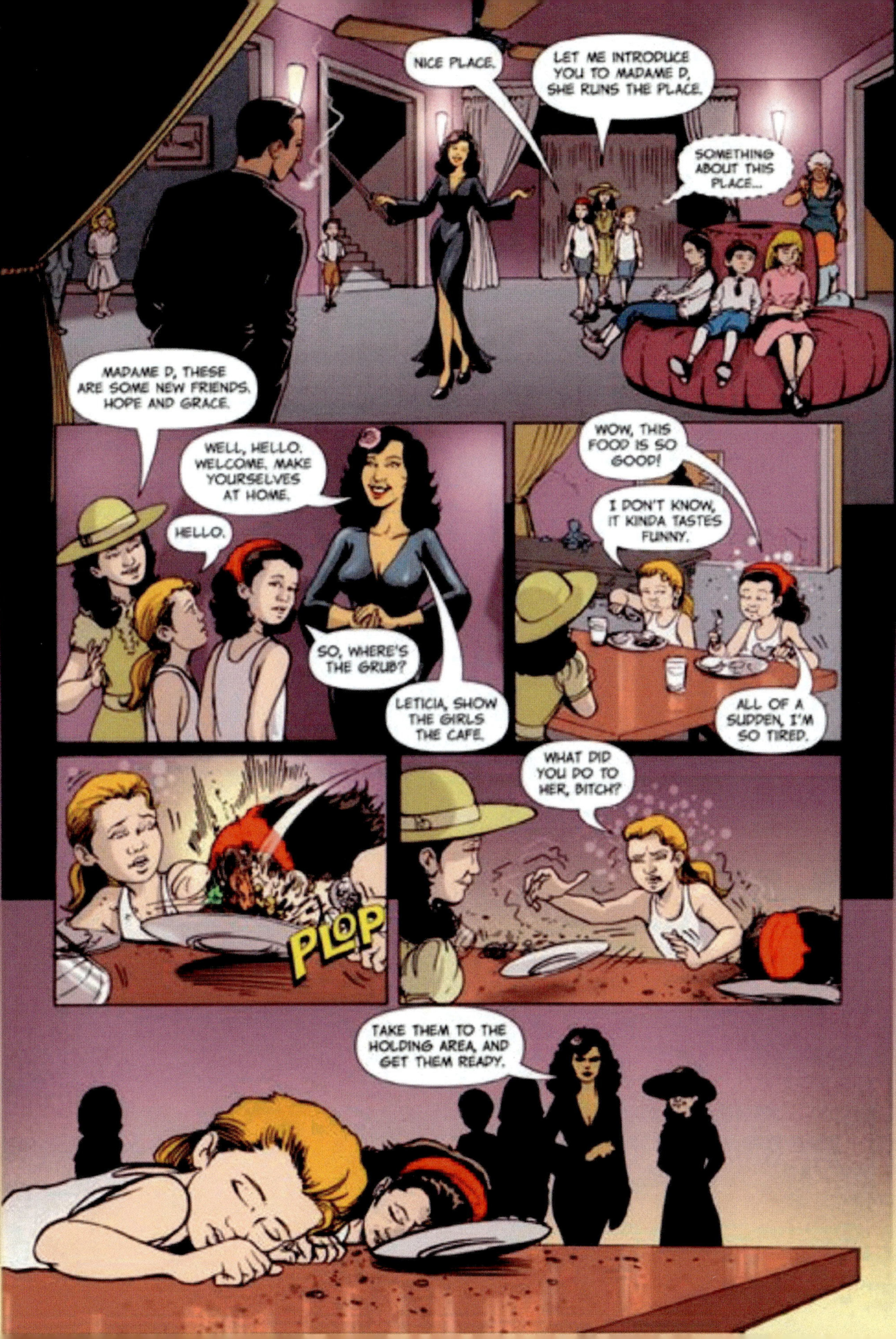
NICE PLACE.
LET ME INTRODUCE YOU TO MADAME D, SHE RUNS THE PLACE.
SOMETHING ABOUT THIS PLACE...
MADAME D, THESE ARE SOME NEW FRIENDS, HOPE AND GRACE.
WELL, HELLO. WELCOME. MAKE YOURSELVES AT HOME.
HELLO.
SO, WHERE'S THE GRUB?
LETICIA, SHOW THE GIRLS THE CAFE.
WOW, THIS FOOD IS SO GOOD!
I DON'T KNOW, IT KINDA TASTES FUNNY.
ALL OF A SUDDEN, I'M SO TIRED.
PLOP
WHAT DID YOU DO TO HER, BITCH?
TAKE THEM TO THE HOLDING AREA, AND GET THEM READY.

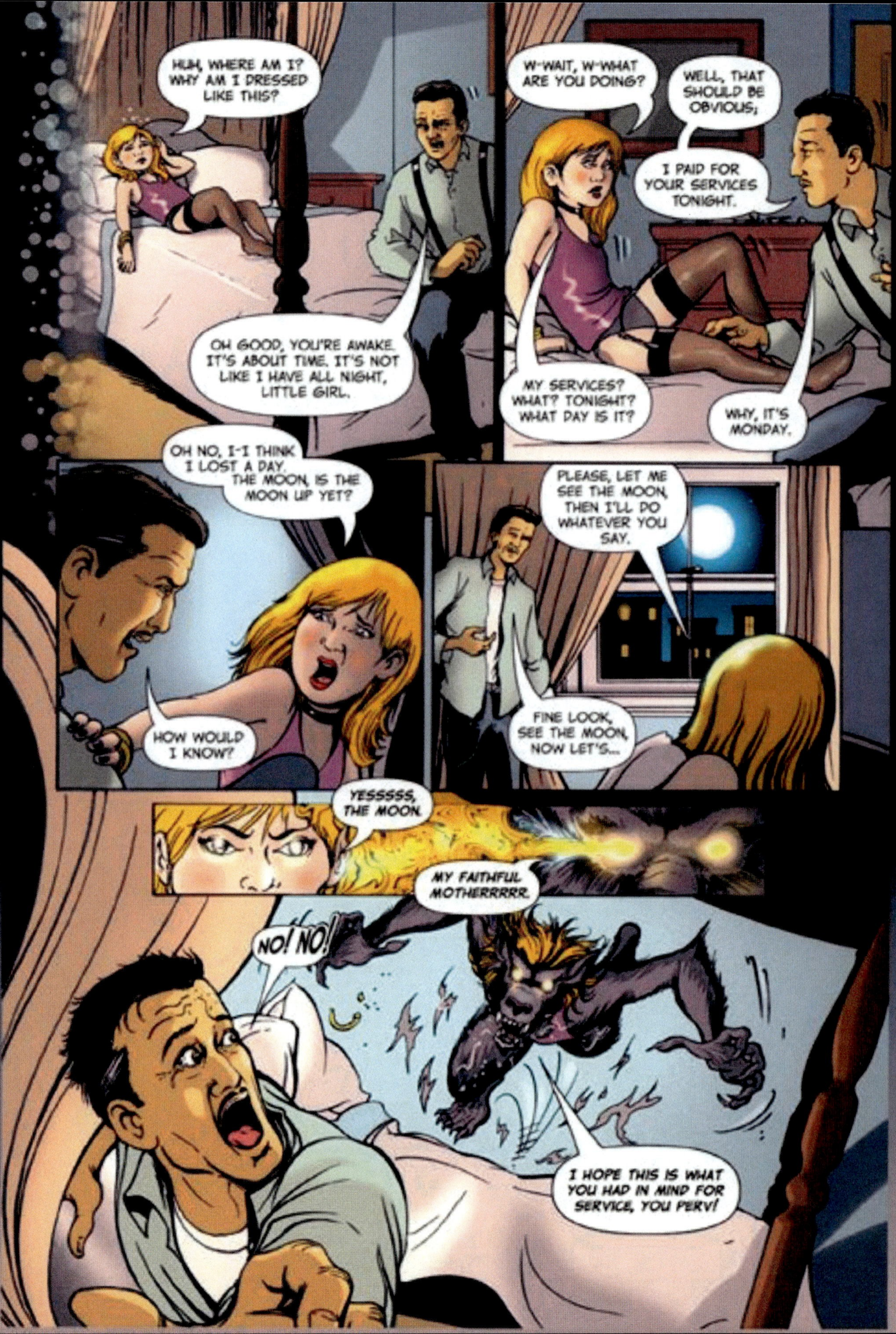
HUH, WHERE AM I? WHY AM I DRESSED LIKE THIS?
OH GOOD, YOU'RE AWAKE. IT'S ABOUT TIME. IT'S NOT LIKE I HAVE ALL NIGHT, LITTLE GIRL.
W-WAIT, W-WHAT ARE YOU DOING?
WELL, THAT SHOULD BE OBVIOUS;
I PAID FOR YOUR SERVICES TONIGHT.
MY SERVICES? WHAT? TONIGHT? WHAT DAY IS IT?
WHY, IT'S MONDAY.
OH NO, I-I THINK I LOST A DAY.
THE MOON, IS THE MOON UP YET?
HOW WOULD I KNOW?
PLEASE, LET ME SEE THE MOON, THEN I'LL DO WHATEVER YOU SAY.
FINE LOOK, SEE THE MOON, NOW LET'S...
YESSSSS, THE MOON.
MY FAITHFUL MOTHERRRRR.
NO! NO!
I HOPE THIS IS WHAT YOU HAD IN MIND FOR SERVICE, YOU PERV!

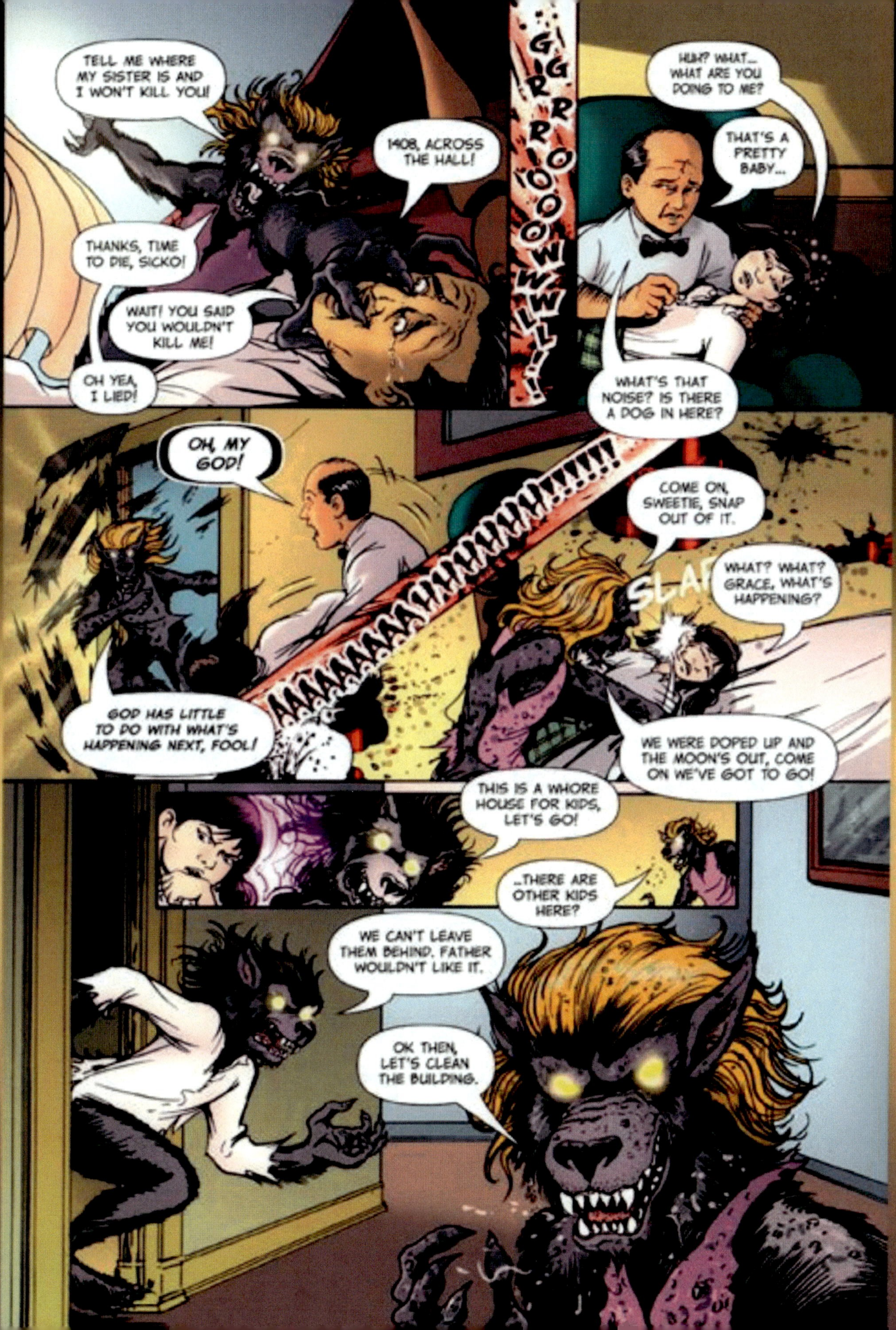
TELL ME WHERE MY SISTER IS AND I WON'T KILL YOU!
1408, ACROSS THE HALL!
THANKS, TIME TO DIE, SICKO!
WAIT! YOU SAID YOU WOULDN'T KILL ME!
OH YEA, I LIED!
GGRRROOOOWWLL!!
HUH? WHAT... WHAT ARE YOU DOING TO ME?
THAT'S A PRETTY BABY...
WHAT'S THAT NOISE? IS THERE A DOG IN HERE?
OH, MY GOD!
AAAAAAAAA!!!!!!!!!!!!!!!!!!!!
GOD HAS LITTLE TO DO WITH WHAT'S HAPPENING NEXT, FOOL!
COME ON, SWEETIE, SNAP OUT OF IT.
SLAP
WHAT? WHAT? GRACE, WHAT'S HAPPENING?
WE WERE DOPED UP AND THE MOON'S OUT, COME ON WE'VE GOT TO GO!
THIS IS A WHORE HOUSE FOR KIDS, LET'S GO!
...THERE ARE OTHER KIDS HERE?
WE CAN'T LEAVE THEM BEHIND. FATHER WOULDN'T LIKE IT.
OK THEN, LET'S CLEAN THE BUILDING.

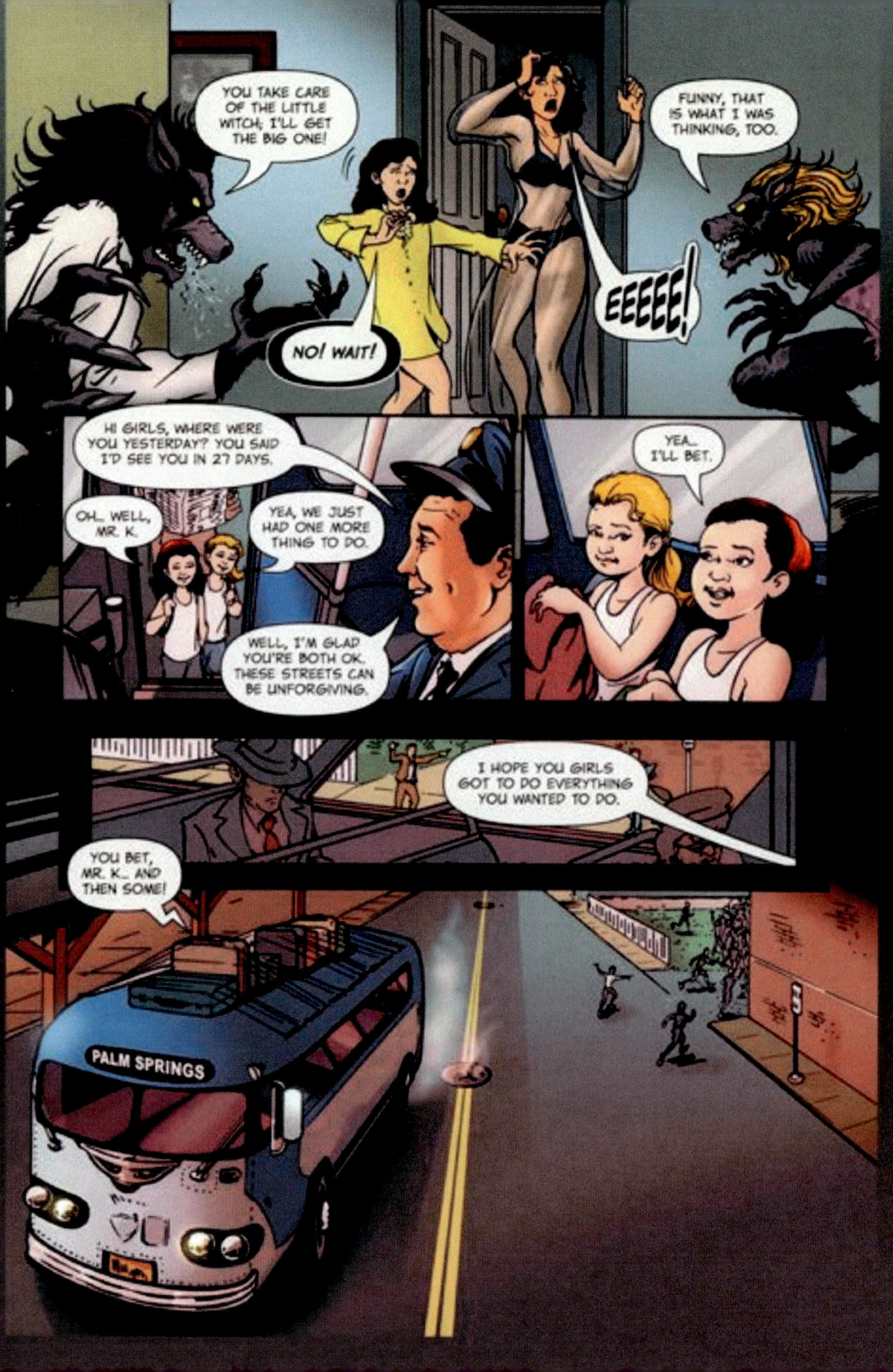
YOU TAKE CARE OF THE LITTLE WITCH; I'LL GET THE BIG ONE!
FUNNY, THAT IS WHAT I WAS THINKING, TOO.
NO! WAIT!
EEEEE!
HI GIRLS, WHERE WERE YOU YESTERDAY? YOU SAID I'D SEE YOU IN 27 DAYS.
OH... WELL, MR. K.
YEA, WE JUST HAD ONE MORE THING TO DO.
WELL, I'M GLAD YOU'RE BOTH OK. THESE STREETS CAN BE UNFORGIVING.
YEA... I'LL BET.
I HOPE YOU GIRLS GOT TO DO EVERYTHING YOU WANTED TO DO.
YOU BET, MR. K... AND THEN SOME!
PALM SPRINGS

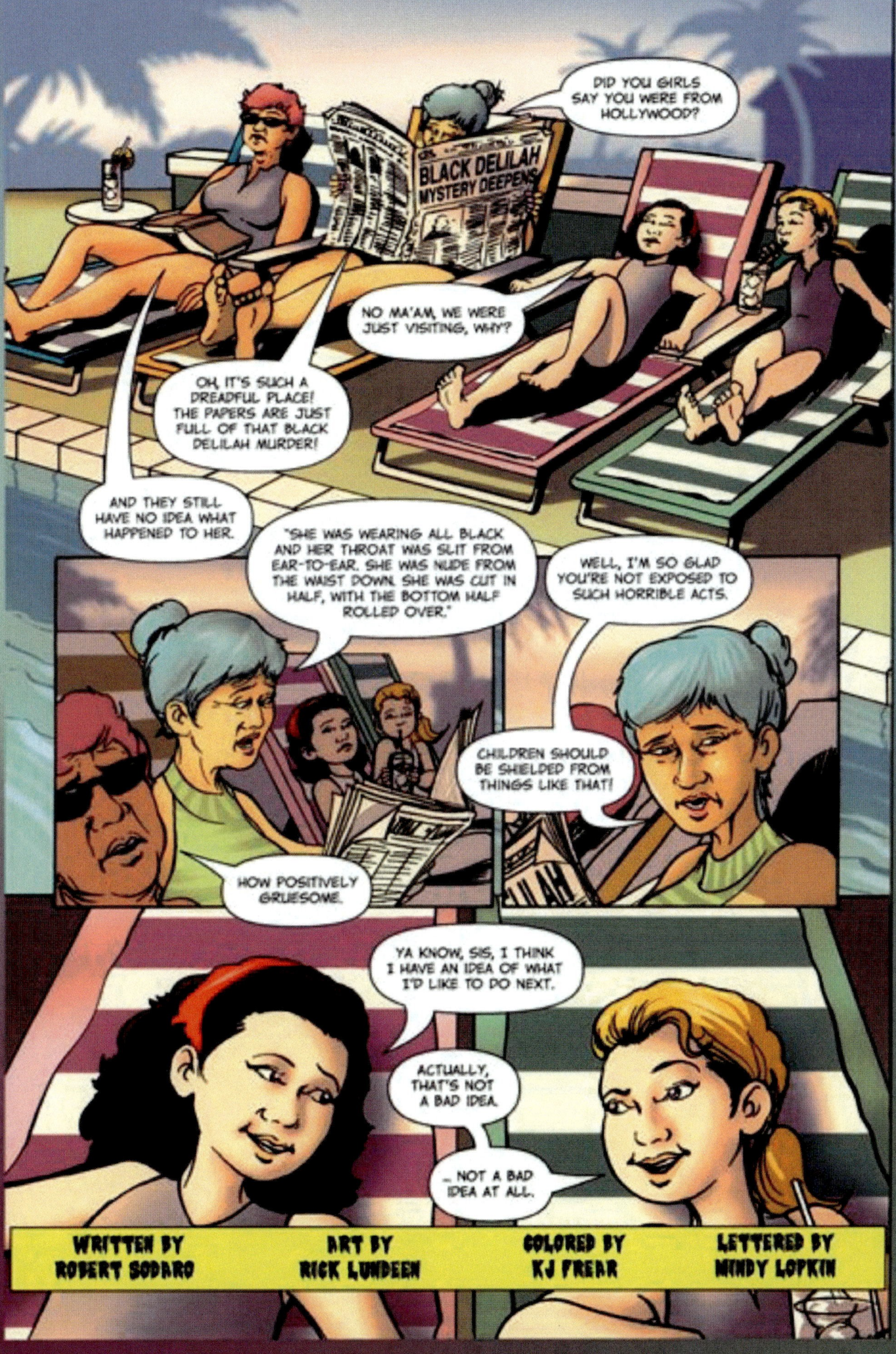
DID YOU GIRLS SAY YOU WERE FROM HOLLYWOOD?
BLACK DELILAH MYSTERY DEEPENS
NO MA'AM, WE WERE JUST VISITING, WHY?
OH, IT'S SUCH A DREADFUL PLACE! THE PAPERS ARE JUST FULL OF THAT BLACK DELILAH MURDER!
AND THEY STILL HAVE NO IDEA WHAT HAPPENED TO HER.
"SHE WAS WEARING ALL BLACK AND HER THROAT WAS SLIT FROM EAR-TO-EAR. SHE WAS NUDE FROM THE WAIST DOWN. SHE WAS CUT IN HALF, WITH THE BOTTOM HALF ROLLED OVER."
HOW POSITIVELY GRUESOME.
WELL, I'M SO GLAD YOU'RE NOT EXPOSED TO SUCH HORRIBLE ACTS.
CHILDREN SHOULD BE SHIELDED FROM THINGS LIKE THAT!
YA KNOW, SIS, I THINK I HAVE AN IDEA OF WHAT I'D LIKE TO DO NEXT.
ACTUALLY, THAT'S NOT A BAD IDEA.
... NOT A BAD IDEA AT ALL.
WRITTEN BY ROBERT SODARO
ART BY RICK LUNDEEN
COLORED BY KJ FREAR
LETTERED BY MINDY LOPKIN

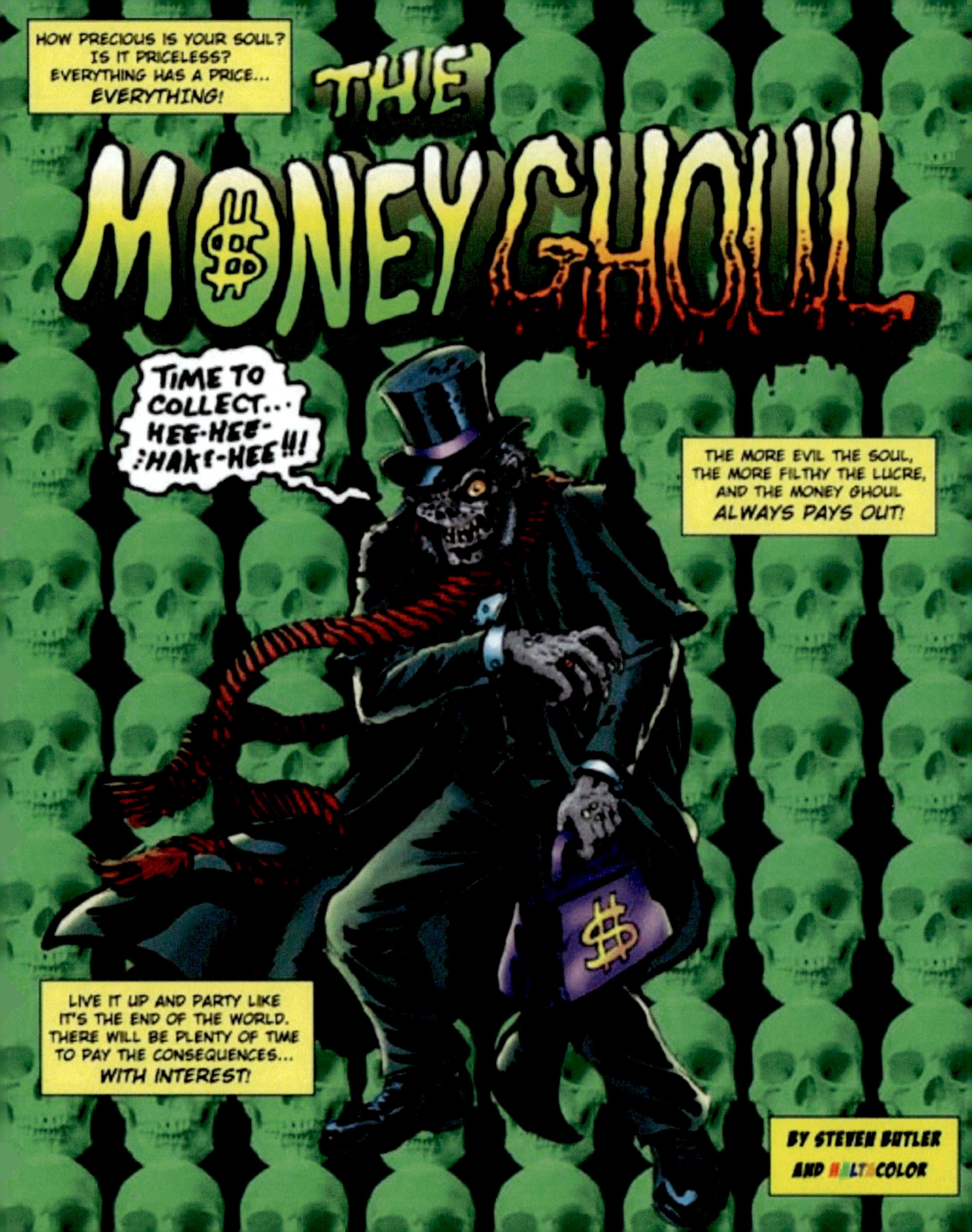
HOW PRECIOUS IS YOUR SOUL? IS IT PRICELESS? EVERYTHING HAS A PRICE... EVERYTHING!
THE MONEY GHOUL
TIME TO COLLECT... HEE-HEE-HAK!-HEE!!!
THE MORE EVIL THE SOUL, THE MORE FILTHY THE LUCRE, AND THE MONEY GHOUL ALWAYS PAYS OUT!
LIVE IT UP AND PARTY LIKE IT'S THE END OF THE WORLD. THERE WILL BE PLENTY OF TIME TO PAY THE CONSEQUENCES... WITH INTEREST!
BY STEVEN BUTLER
AND

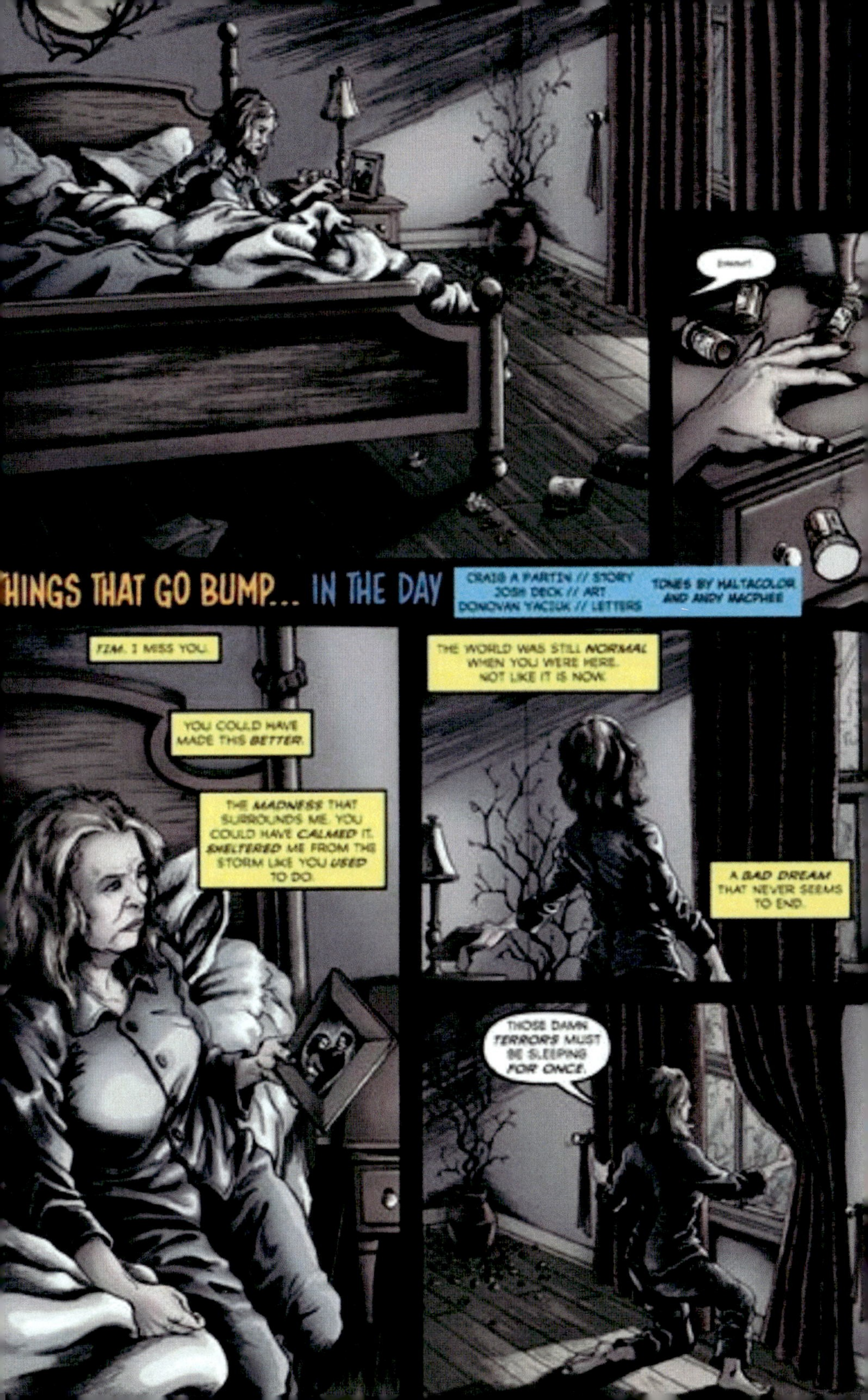
THINGS THAT GO BUMP... IN THE DAY
CRAIG A PARTIN // STORY
JOSH DECK // ART
DONOVAN YACIUK // LETTERS
TONES BY HALTACOLOR AND ANDY MACPHEE
TIM. I MISS YOU.
YOU COULD HAVE MADE THIS BETTER.
THE MADNESS THAT SURROUNDS ME. YOU COULD HAVE CALMED IT. SHELTERED ME FROM THE STORM LIKE YOU USED TO DO.
THE WORLD WAS STILL NORMAL WHEN YOU WERE HERE. NOT LIKE IT IS NOW.
A BAD DREAM THAT NEVER SEEMS TO END.
THOSE DAMN TERRORS MUST BE SLEEPING FOR ONCE.

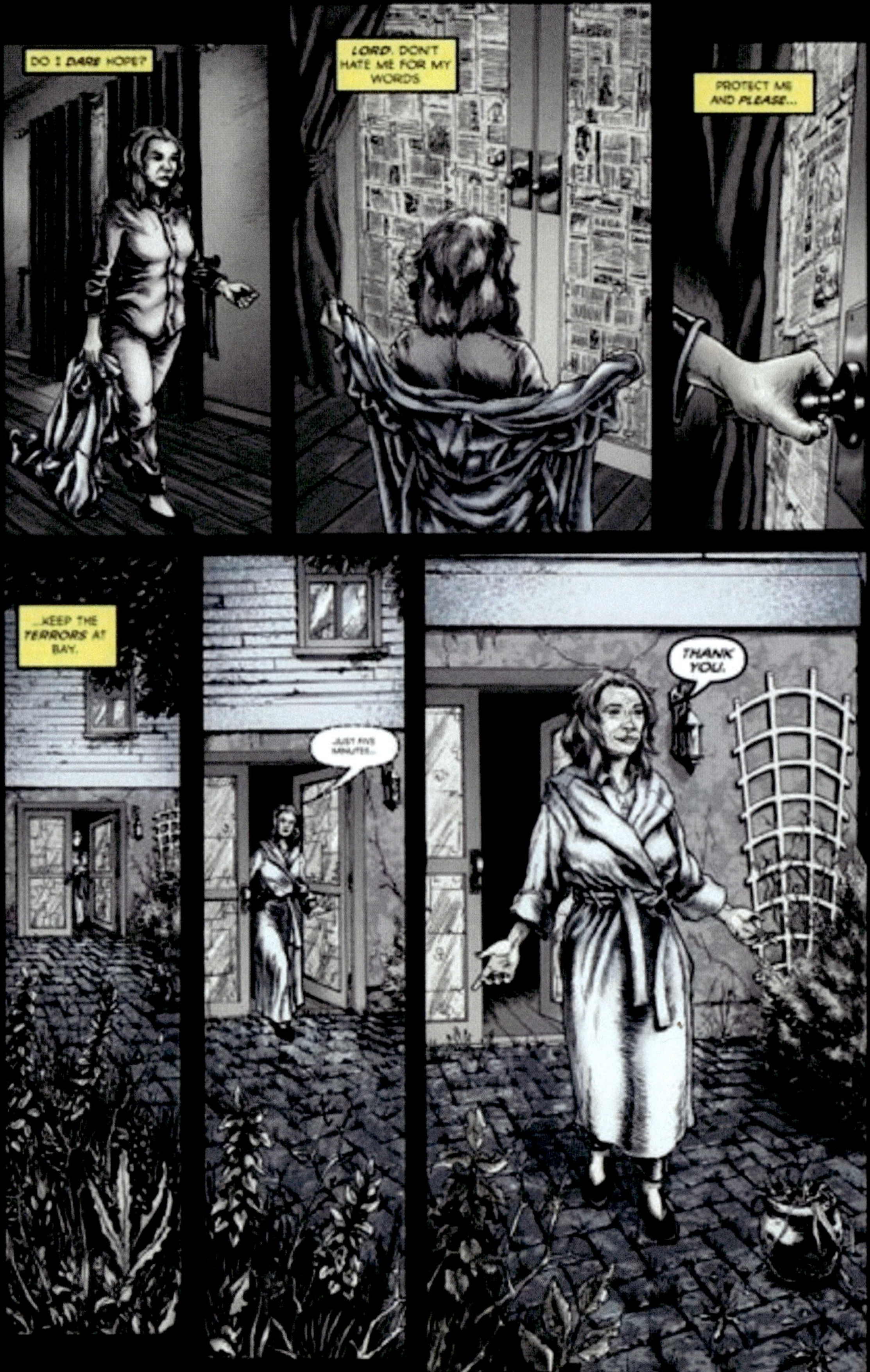
DO I DARE HOPE?
LORD, DON'T HATE ME FOR MY WORDS
PROTECT ME AND PLEASE...
...KEEP THE TERRORS AT BAY.
JUST FIVE MINUTES...
THANK YOU.

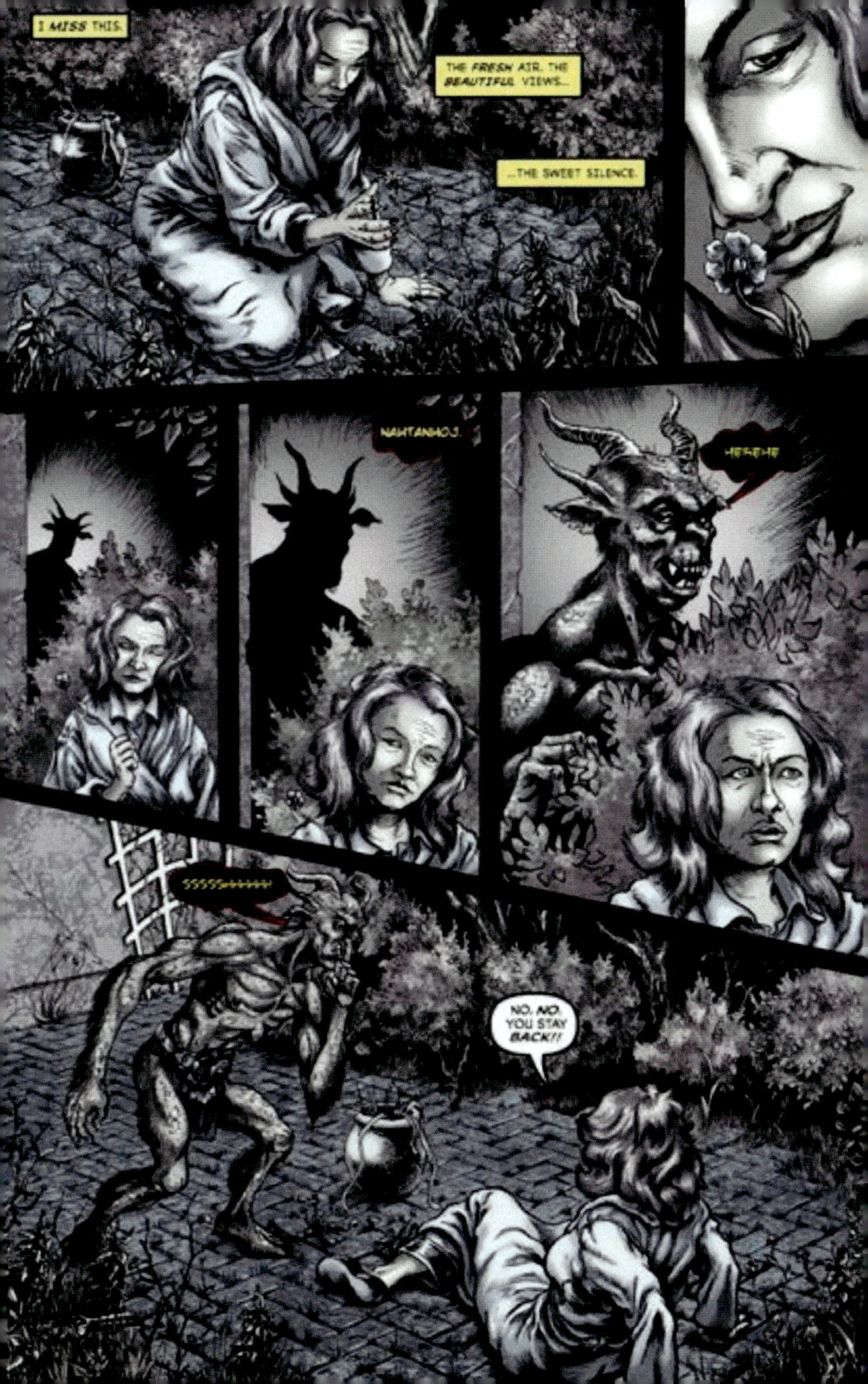
I MISS THIS.
THE FRESH AIR. THE BEAUTIFUL VIEWS...
...THE SWEET SILENCE.
NAHTANHOJ.
HEHEHE
SSSSSHHHHH
NO. NO. YOU STAY BACK!!

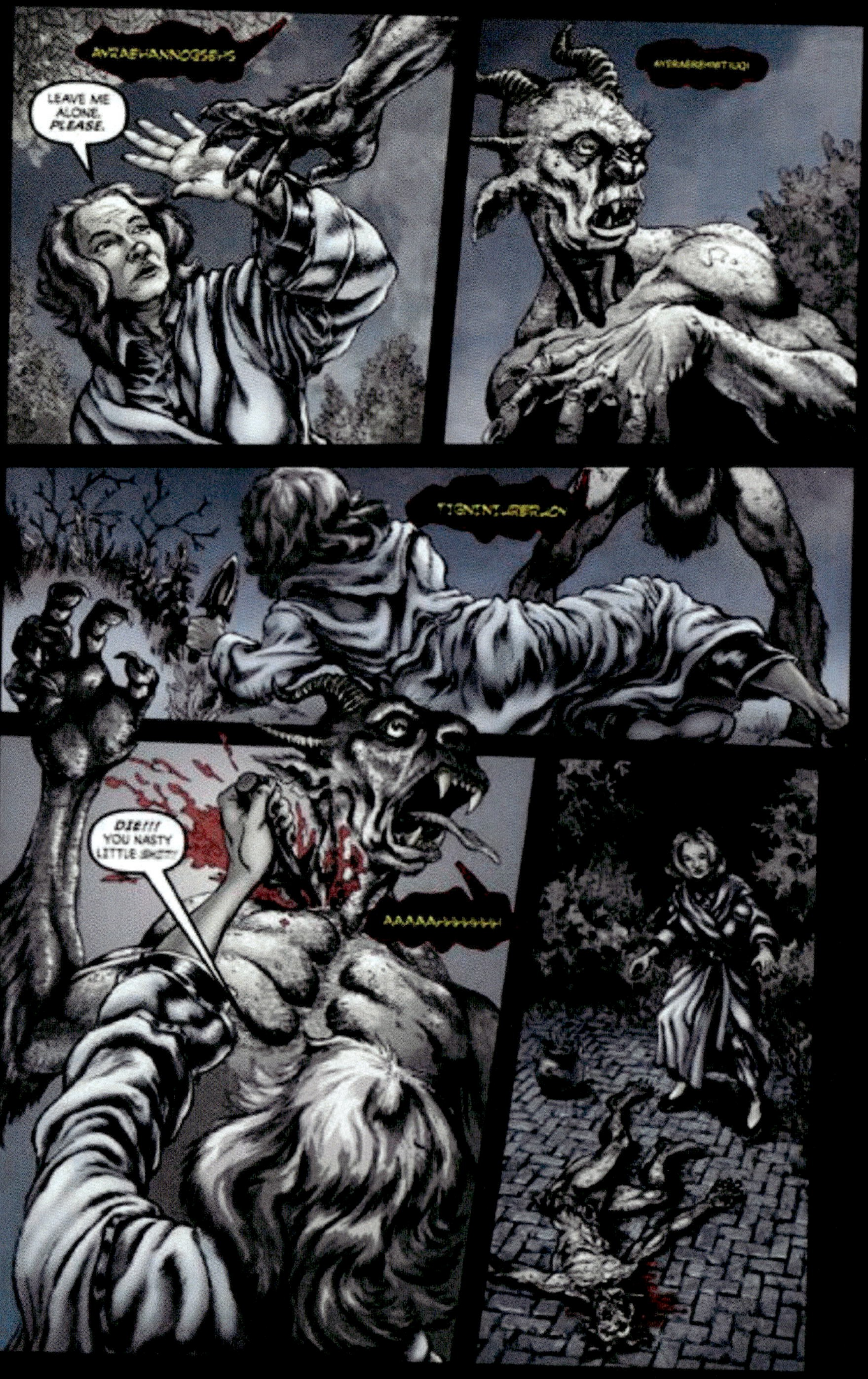
LEAVE ME ALONE. *PLEASE.*
DIE!!! YOU NASTY LITTLE *SHIT!!*
AAAAA-HHHHHH

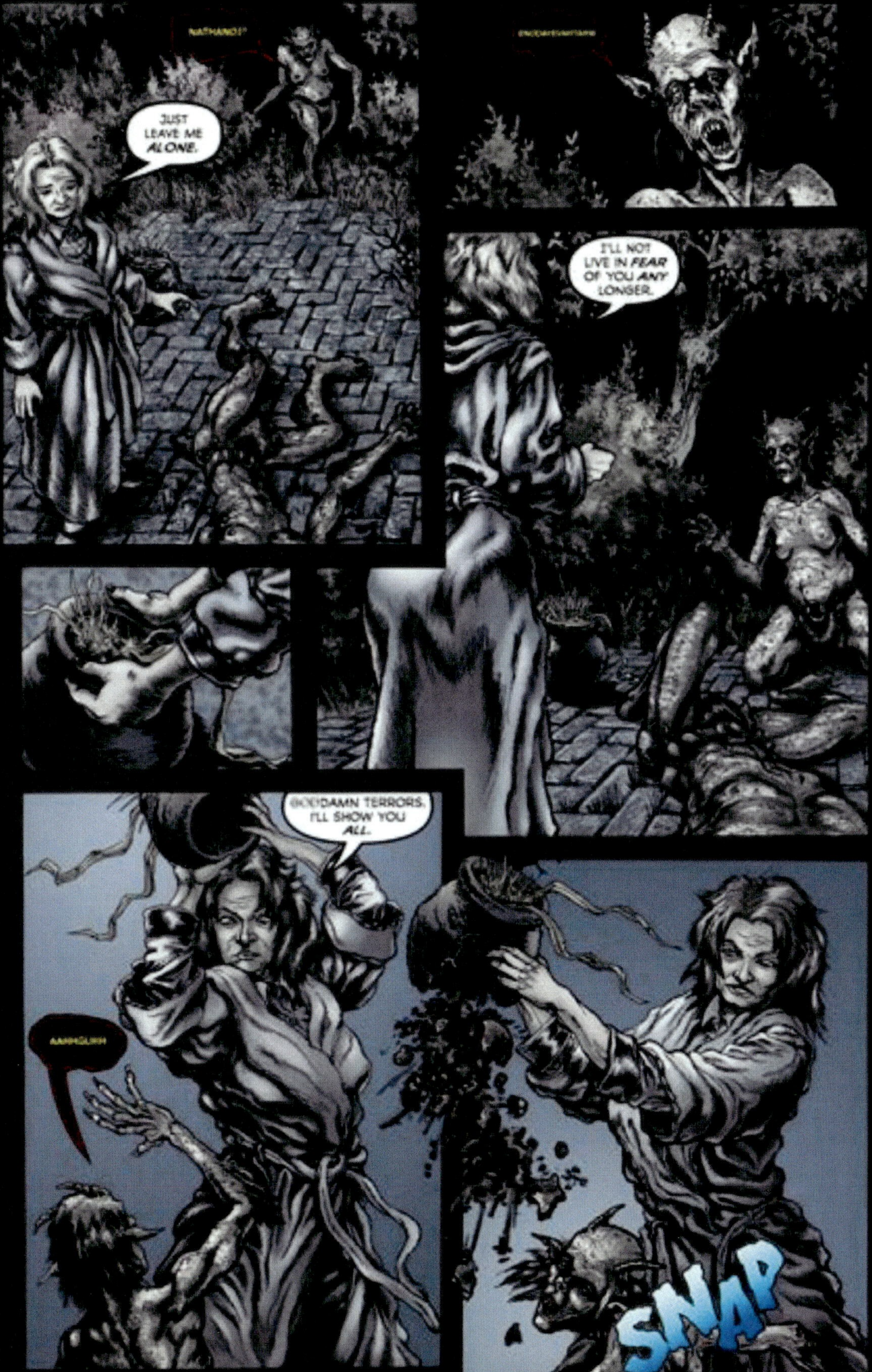
NATHANOS!?
JUST LEAVE ME ALONE.
I'LL NOT LIVE IN FEAR OF YOU ANY LONGER.
GODDAMN TERRORS. I'LL SHOW YOU ALL.
AAHHGURH
SNAP

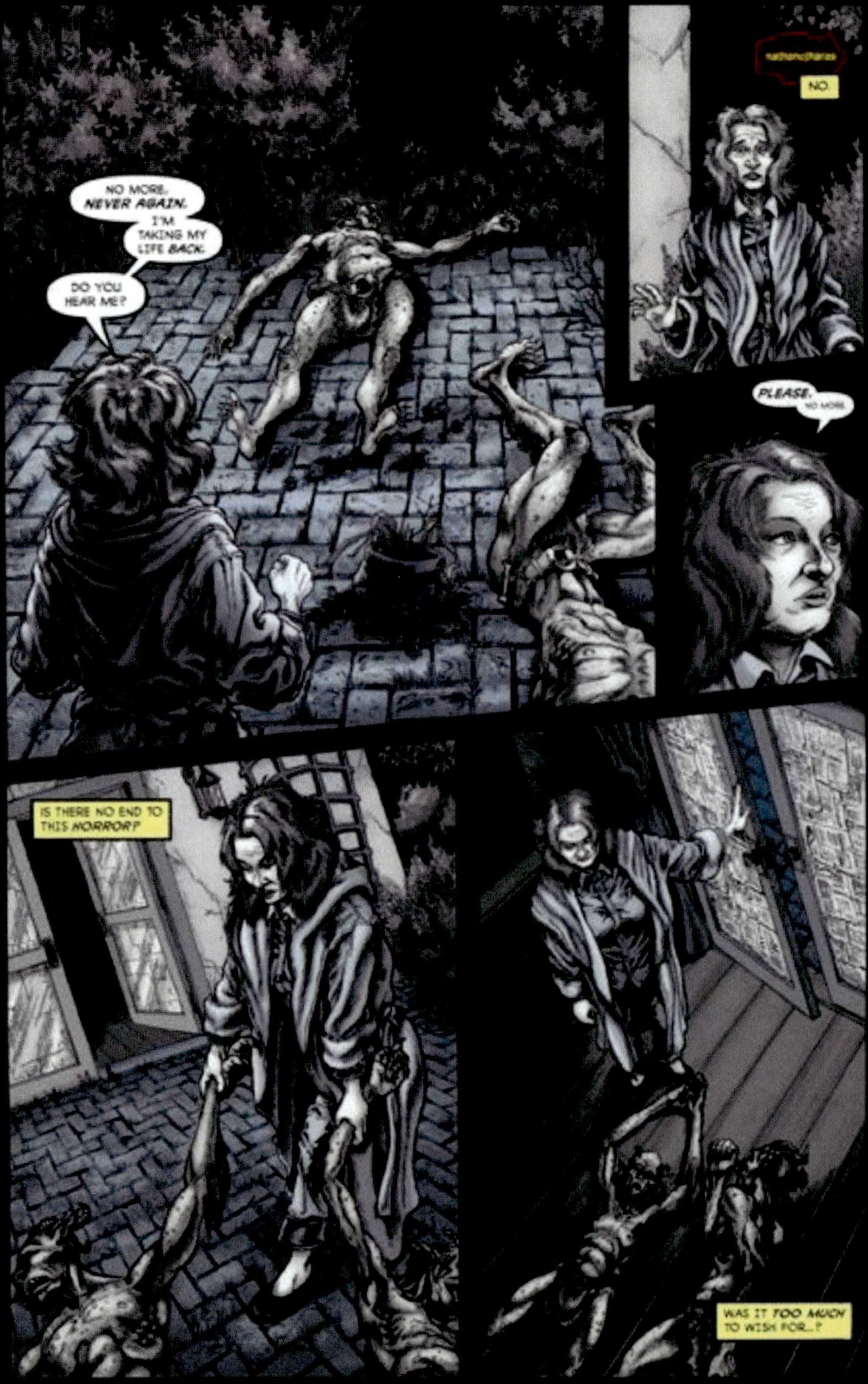
NO MORE. NEVER AGAIN.
I'M TAKING MY LIFE BACK.
DO YOU HEAR ME?
NO.
PLEASE.
NO MORE.
IS THERE NO END TO THIS HORROR?
WAS IT TOO MUCH TO WISH FOR...?

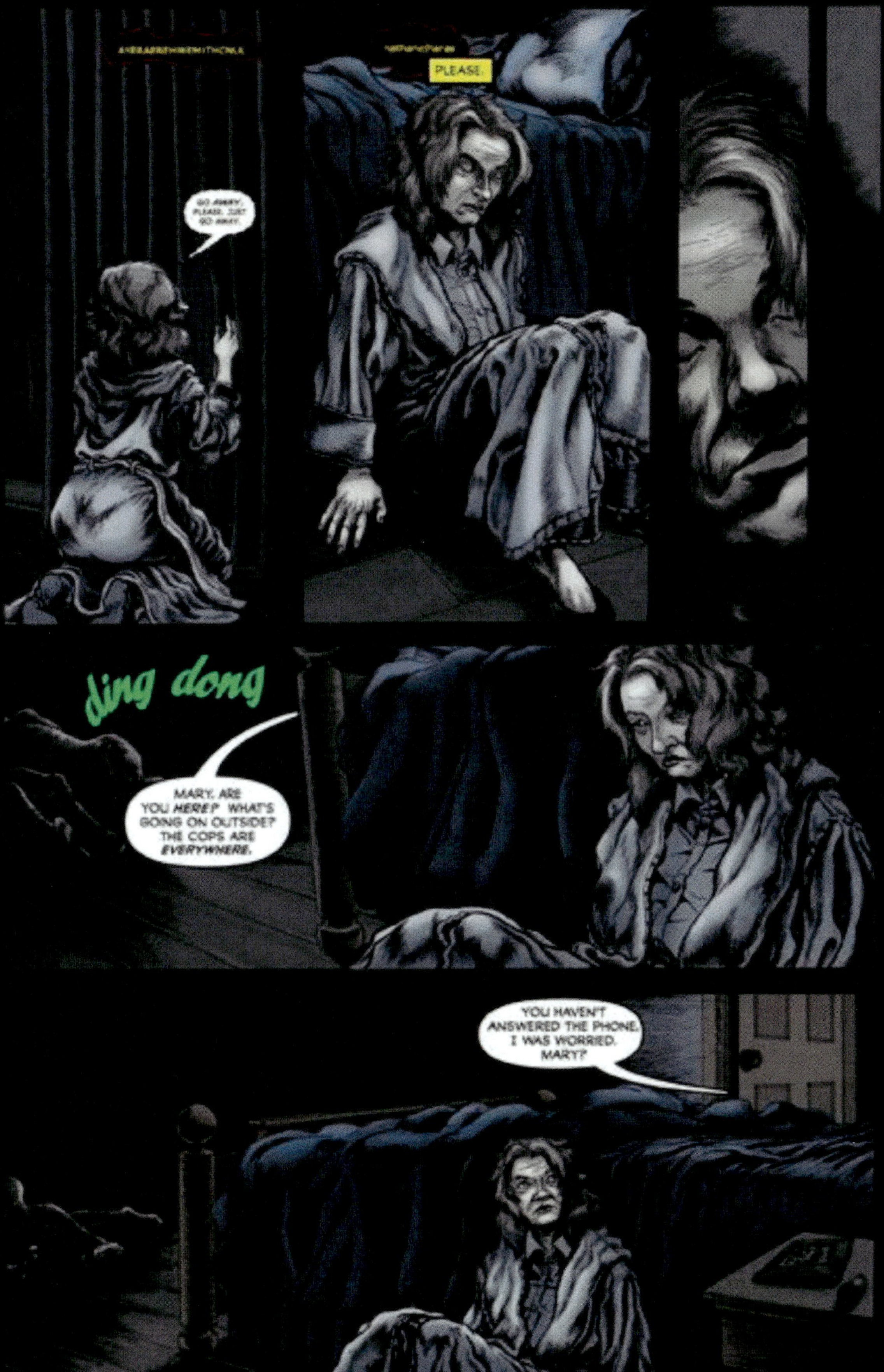
PLEASE.
GO AWAY. PLEASE. JUST GO AWAY.
ding dong
MARY, ARE YOU *HERE?* WHAT'S GOING ON OUTSIDE? THE COPS ARE *EVERYWHERE.*
YOU HAVEN'T ANSWERED THE PHONE. I WAS WORRIED. MARY?

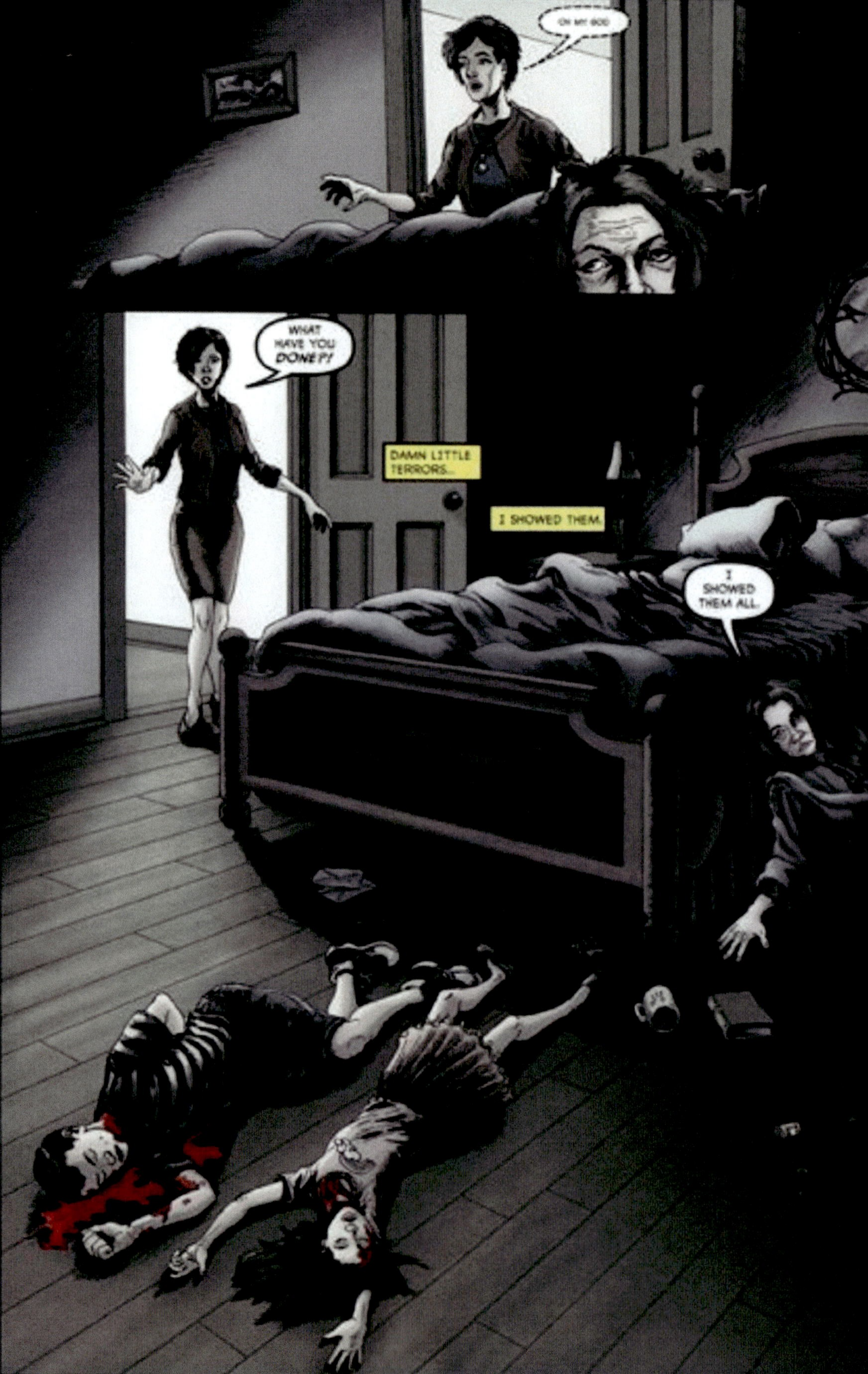
OH MY GOD
WHAT HAVE YOU *DONE?!*
DAMN LITTLE TERRORS...
I SHOWED THEM.
I SHOWED THEM ALL.

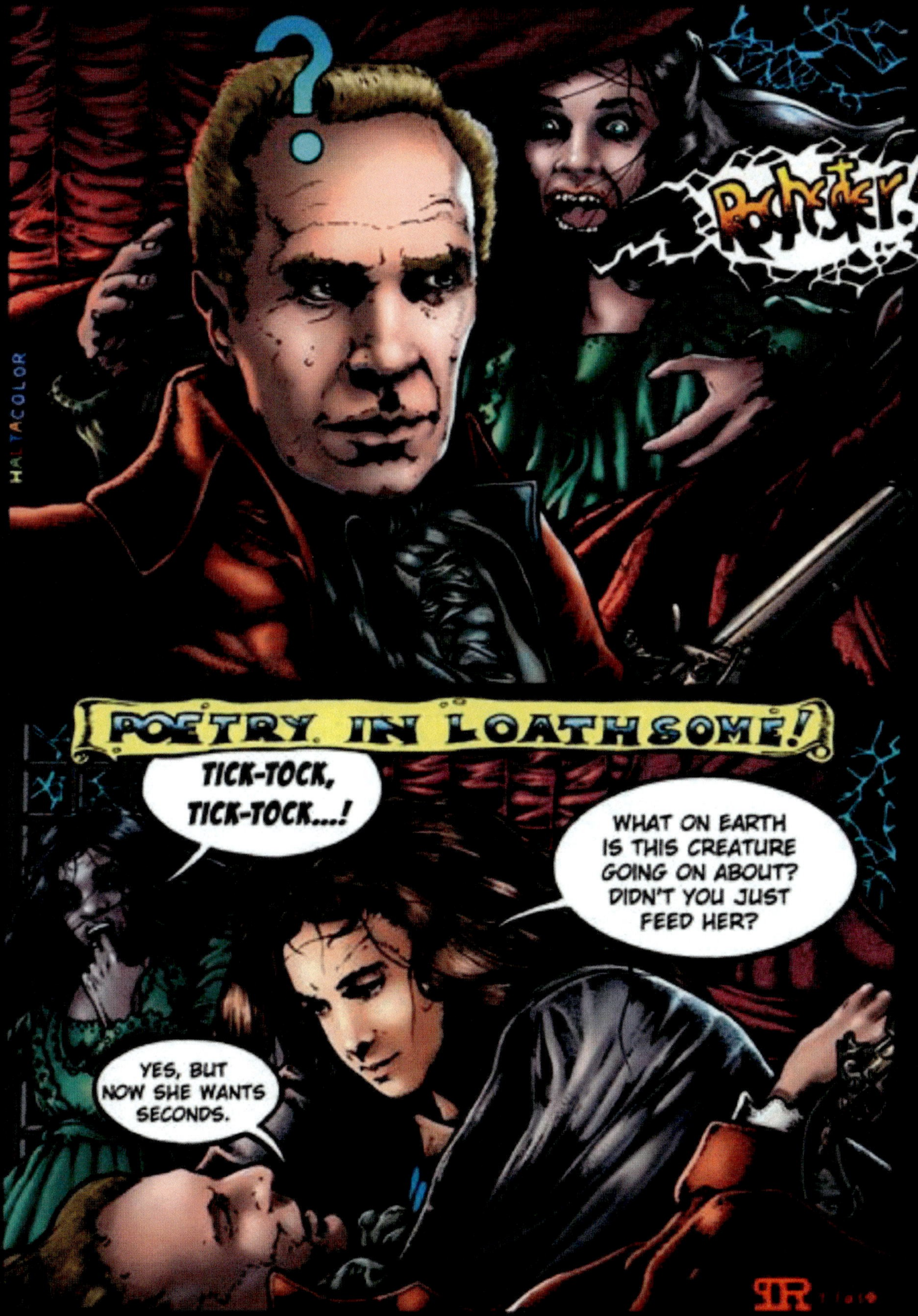
?
Rochester!
POETRY IN LOATHSOME!
TICK-TOCK, TICK-TOCK...!
WHAT ON EARTH IS THIS CREATURE GOING ON ABOUT? DIDN'T YOU JUST FEED HER?
YES, BUT NOW SHE WANTS SECONDS.

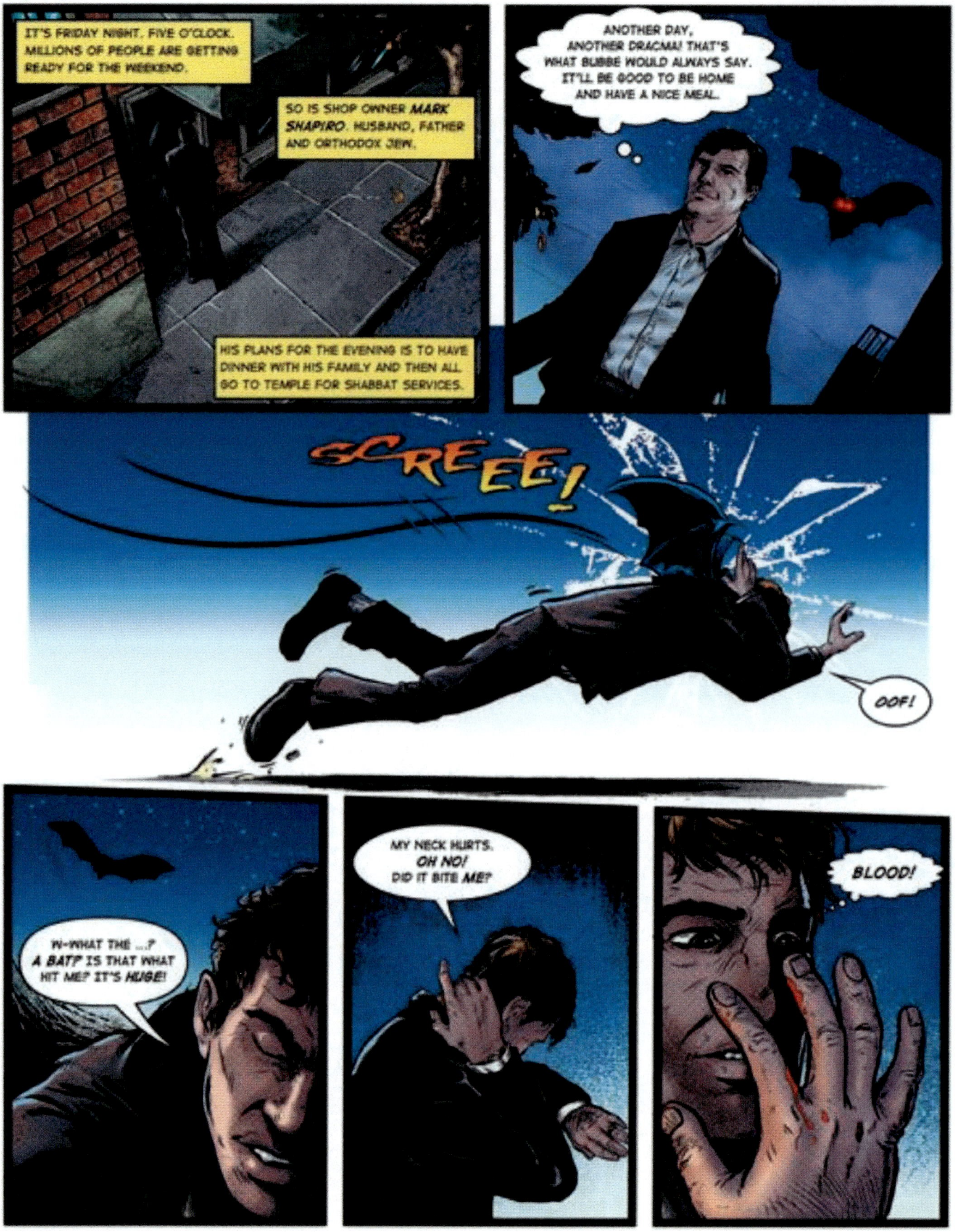
IT'S FRIDAY NIGHT. FIVE O'CLOCK. MILLIONS OF PEOPLE ARE GETTING READY FOR THE WEEKEND.
SO IS SHOP OWNER MARK SHAPIRO. HUSBAND, FATHER AND ORTHODOX JEW.
HIS PLANS FOR THE EVENING IS TO HAVE DINNER WITH HIS FAMILY AND THEN ALL GO TO TEMPLE FOR SHABBAT SERVICES.
ANOTHER DAY, ANOTHER DRACMA! THAT'S WHAT BUBBE WOULD ALWAYS SAY. IT'LL BE GOOD TO BE HOME AND HAVE A NICE MEAL.
SCREEE!
OOF!
W-WHAT THE ...? A BAT? IS THAT WHAT HIT ME? IT'S HUGE!
MY NECK HURTS. OH NO! DID IT BITE ME?
BLOOD!

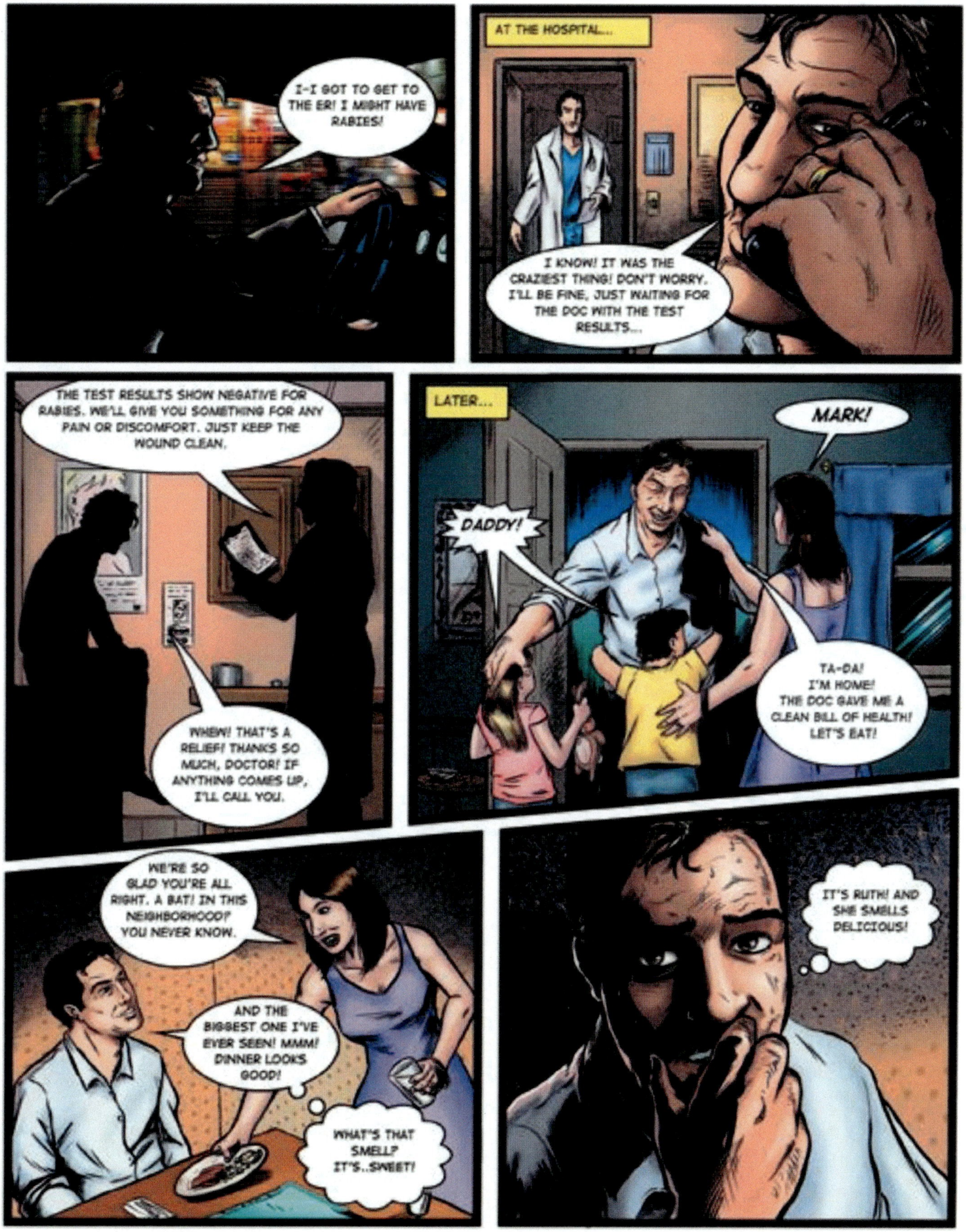
I-I GOT TO GET TO THE ER! I MIGHT HAVE RABIES!
AT THE HOSPITAL...
I KNOW! IT WAS THE CRAZIEST THING! DON'T WORRY. I'LL BE FINE, JUST WAITING FOR THE DOC WITH THE TEST RESULTS...
THE TEST RESULTS SHOW NEGATIVE FOR RABIES. WE'LL GIVE YOU SOMETHING FOR ANY PAIN OR DISCOMFORT. JUST KEEP THE WOUND CLEAN.
WHEW! THAT'S A RELIEF! THANKS SO MUCH, DOCTOR! IF ANYTHING COMES UP, I'LL CALL YOU.
LATER...
MARK!
DADDY!
TA-DA! I'M HOME! THE DOC GAVE ME A CLEAN BILL OF HEALTH! LET'S EAT!
WE'RE SO GLAD YOU'RE ALL RIGHT. A BAT! IN THIS NEIGHBORHOOD? YOU NEVER KNOW.
AND THE BIGGEST ONE I'VE EVER SEEN! MMM! DINNER LOOKS GOOD!
WHAT'S THAT SMELL? IT'S..SWEET!
IT'S RUTH! AND SHE SMELLS DELICIOUS!

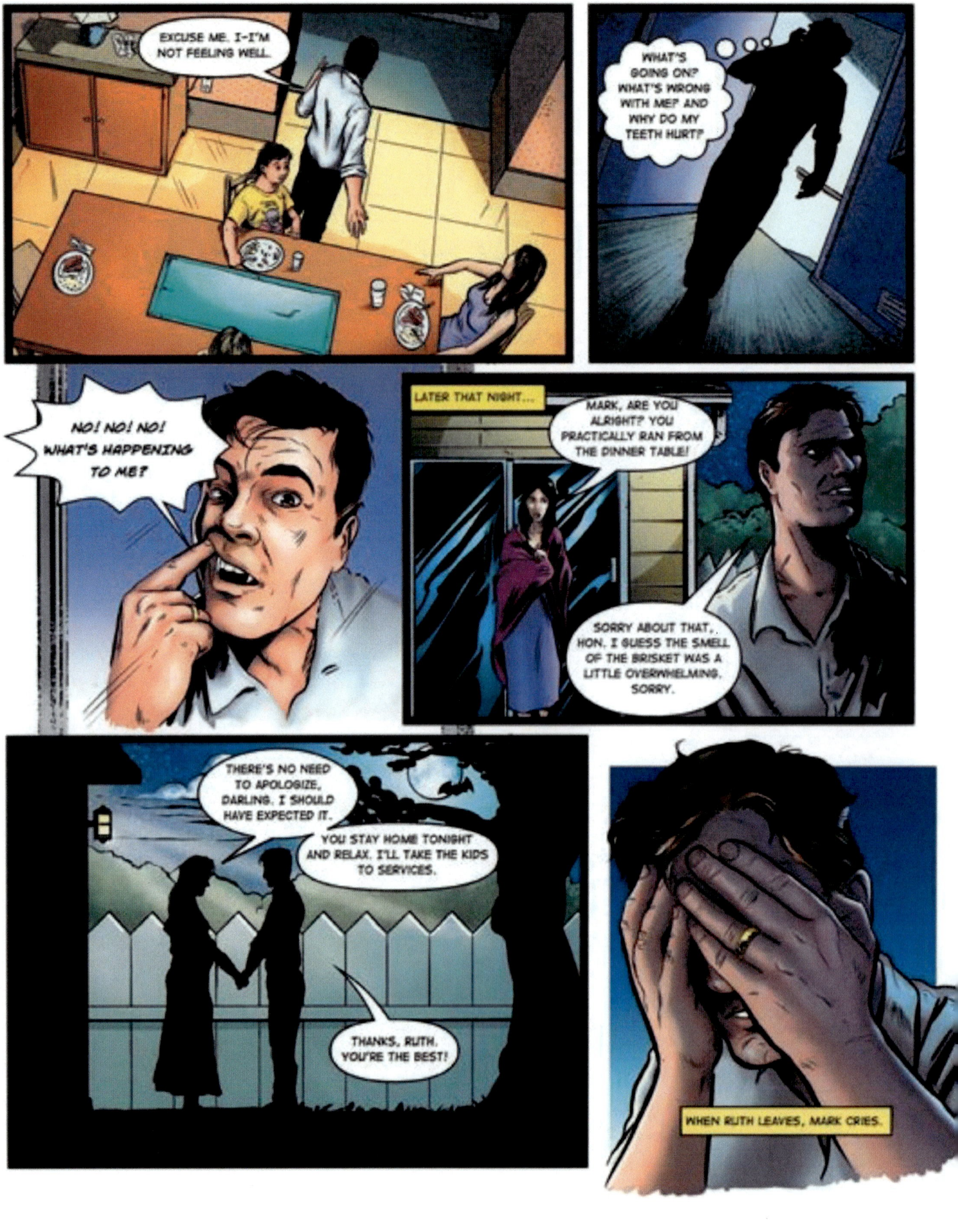
EXCUSE ME. I-I'M NOT FEELING WELL.
WHAT'S GOING ON? WHAT'S WRONG WITH ME? AND WHY DO MY TEETH HURT?
NO! NO! NO! WHAT'S HAPPENING TO ME?
LATER THAT NIGHT...
MARK, ARE YOU ALRIGHT? YOU PRACTICALLY RAN FROM THE DINNER TABLE!
SORRY ABOUT THAT, HON. I GUESS THE SMELL OF THE BRISKET WAS A LITTLE OVERWHELMING. SORRY.
THERE'S NO NEED TO APOLOGIZE, DARLING. I SHOULD HAVE EXPECTED IT.
YOU STAY HOME TONIGHT AND RELAX. I'LL TAKE THE KIDS TO SERVICES.
THANKS, RUTH. YOU'RE THE BEST!
WHEN RUTH LEAVES, MARK CRIES.

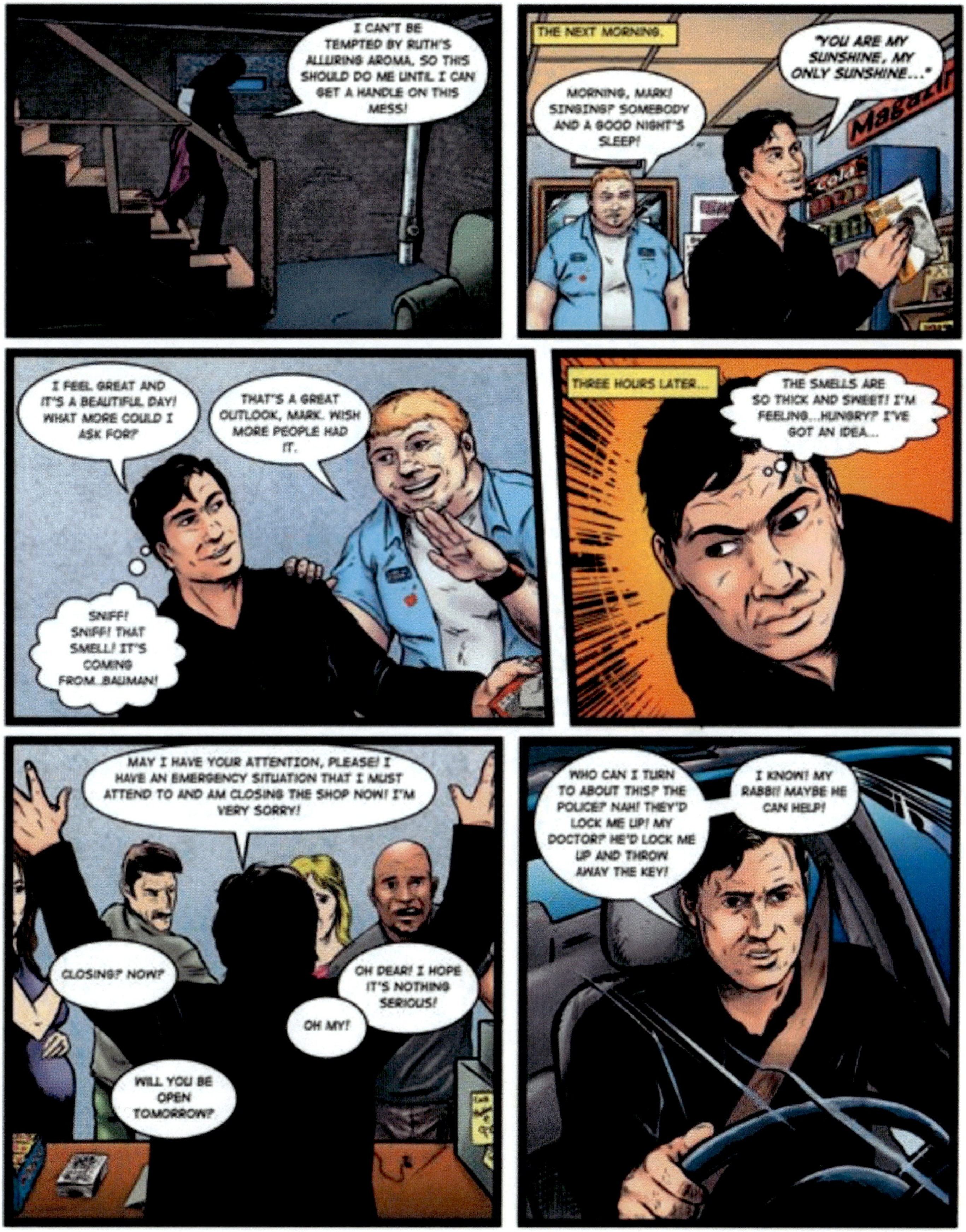
I CAN'T BE TEMPTED BY RUTH'S ALLURING AROMA, SO THIS SHOULD DO ME UNTIL I CAN GET A HANDLE ON THIS MESS!
THE NEXT MORNING.
"YOU ARE MY SUNSHINE, MY ONLY SUNSHINE..."
MORNING, MARK! SINGING? SOMEBODY HAD A GOOD NIGHT'S SLEEP!
I FEEL GREAT AND IT'S A BEAUTIFUL DAY! WHAT MORE COULD I ASK FOR?
THAT'S A GREAT OUTLOOK, MARK. WISH MORE PEOPLE HAD IT.
SNIFF! SNIFF! THAT SMELL! IT'S COMING FROM...BAUMAN!
THREE HOURS LATER...
THE SMELLS ARE SO THICK AND SWEET! I'M FEELING...HUNGRY? I'VE GOT AN IDEA...
MAY I HAVE YOUR ATTENTION, PLEASE! I HAVE AN EMERGENCY SITUATION THAT I MUST ATTEND TO AND AM CLOSING THE SHOP NOW! I'M VERY SORRY!
CLOSING? NOW?
OH DEAR! I HOPE IT'S NOTHING SERIOUS!
OH MY!
WILL YOU BE OPEN TOMORROW?
WHO CAN I TURN TO ABOUT THIS? THE POLICE? NAH! THEY'D LOCK ME UP! MY DOCTOR? HE'D LOCK ME UP AND THROW AWAY THE KEY!
I KNOW! MY RABBI! MAYBE HE CAN HELP!

SOON...

HELLO. I WAS WONDERING IF I MIGHT BE ABLE TO SEE THE RABBI TODAY?

YOU'RE IN LUCK! HE'S IN HIS OFFICE. JUST KNOCK BEFORE ENTERING.

THANK YOU.

MARK! ALWAYS A PLEASURE TO SEE YOU! SIT! SIT! WHAT CAN I DO FOR YOU TODAY?

I HAVE A STORY TO TELL YOU AND I HOPE YOU WON'T THINK ME CRAZY!

FIFTEEN MINUTES LATER...

AND THAT'S THE TRUTH, RABBI! SO HELP ME!

YOUR STORY IS THE THIRD ONE I'VE HEARD THIS YEAR! WEIS AND BECK WERE ATTACKED AS WELL. THE LEGEND OF THE VAMPIRE IS REAL, AS YOU NOW KNOW, MARK.

YOU ARE NOW FACING CHANGES IN YOUR LIFE. DRASTIC CHANGES. THE FIRST AND MOST IMPORTANT CHANGE WILL COME WITH YOUR FAMILY.

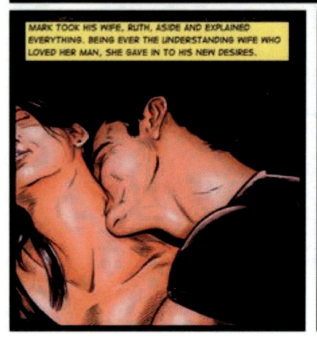

MARK TOOK HIS WIFE, RUTH, ASIDE AND EXPLAINED EVERYTHING. BEING EVER THE UNDERSTANDING WIFE WHO LOVED HER MAN, SHE GAVE IN TO HIS NEW DESIRES.

IT DIDN'T STOP THERE. SOON THE WHOLE SHAPIRO FAMILY WAS "ONE" WITH FATHER.

THE CHILDREN WERE NOW HOME SCHOOLED.

THE FAMILY COULD VENTURE OUTSIDE, THANKS TO RUTH'S HOMEMADE SUNBLOCK., SPF 500+!

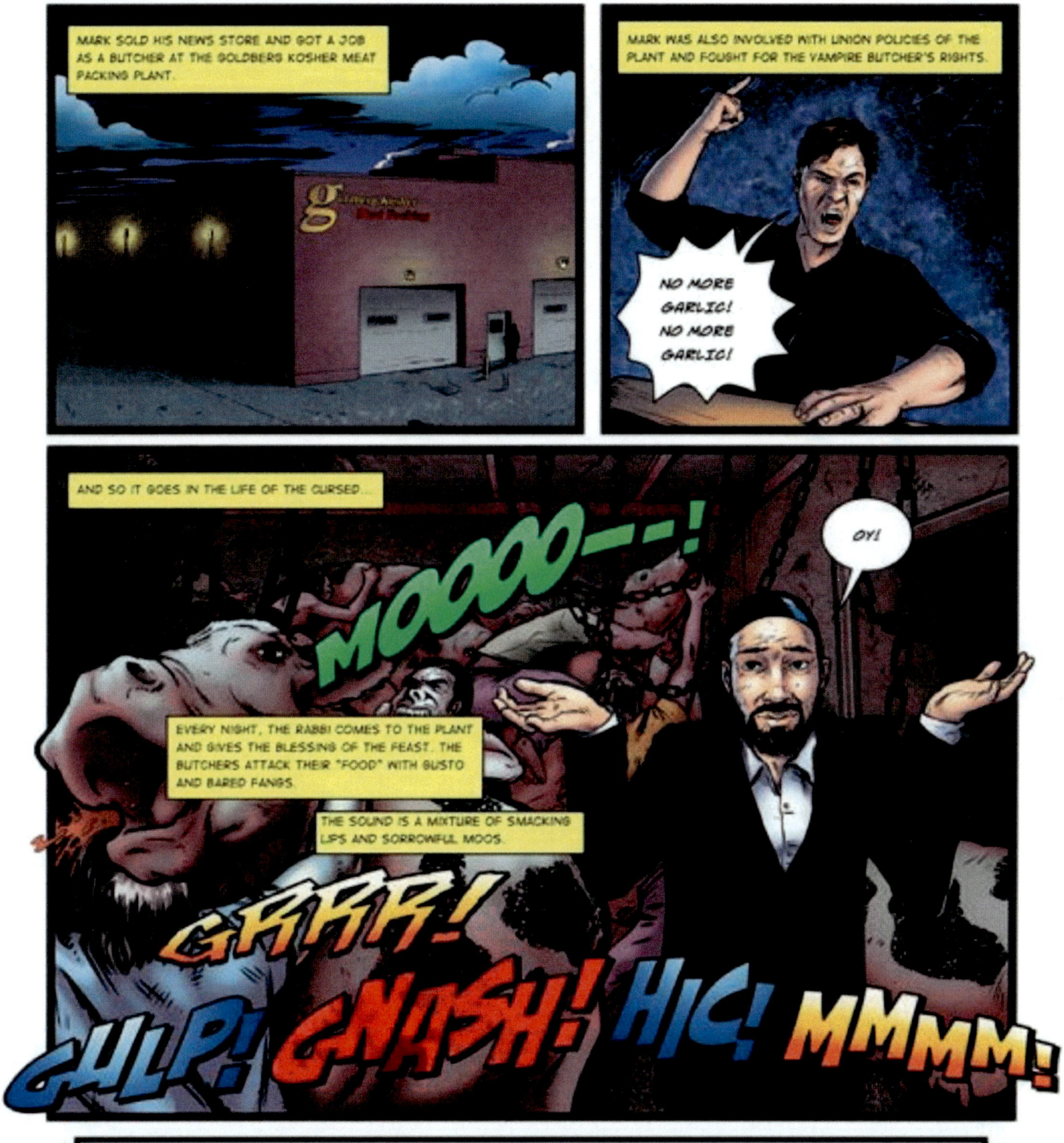
MARK SOLD HIS NEWS STORE AND GOT A JOB AS A BUTCHER AT THE GOLDBERG KOSHER MEAT PACKING PLANT.
MARK WAS ALSO INVOLVED WITH UNION POLICIES OF THE PLANT AND FOUGHT FOR THE VAMPIRE BUTCHER'S RIGHTS.
NO MORE GARLIC! NO MORE GARLIC!
AND SO IT GOES IN THE LIFE OF THE CURSED...
MOOOO--!
OY!
EVERY NIGHT, THE RABBI COMES TO THE PLANT AND GIVES THE BLESSING OF THE FEAST. THE BUTCHERS ATTACK THEIR "FOOD" WITH GUSTO AND BARED FANGS.
THE SOUND IS A MIXTURE OF SMACKING LIPS AND SORROWFUL MOOS.
GRRR!
GULP! GNASH! HIC! MMMM!

MARK, OF THE VAMPIRES

WRITTEN BY DAN SMEDDY
ART BY KEVIN J. FREAR
COLORS BY KEVIN S. HALTER

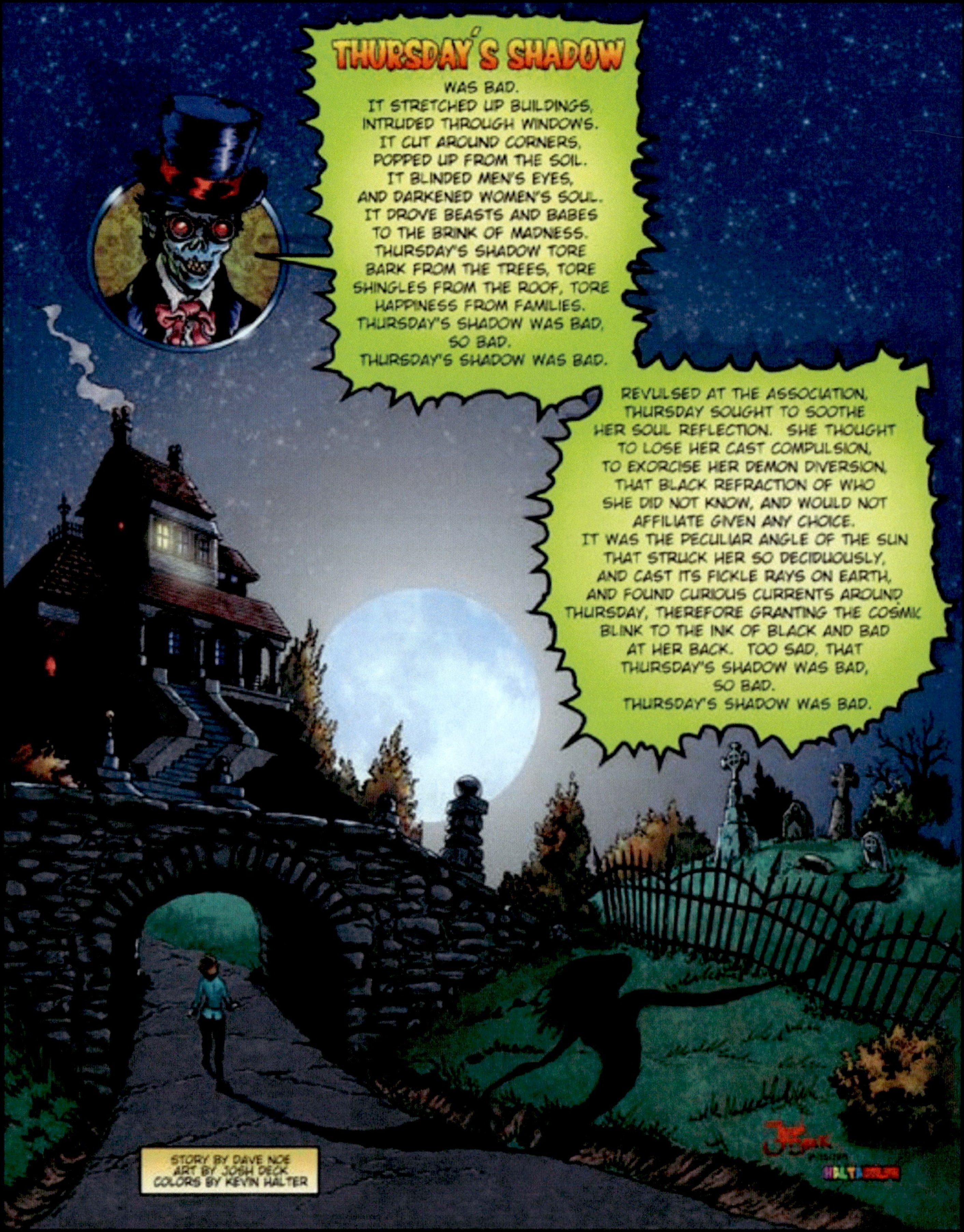
THURSDAY'S SHADOW
WAS BAD. IT STRETCHED UP BUILDINGS, INTRUDED THROUGH WINDOWS. IT CUT AROUND CORNERS, POPPED UP FROM THE SOIL. IT BLINDED MEN'S EYES, AND DARKENED WOMEN'S SOUL. IT DROVE BEASTS AND BABES TO THE BRINK OF MADNESS. THURSDAY'S SHADOW TORE BARK FROM THE TREES, TORE SHINGLES FROM THE ROOF, TORE HAPPINESS FROM FAMILIES. THURSDAY'S SHADOW WAS BAD, SO BAD. THURSDAY'S SHADOW WAS BAD.
REVULSED AT THE ASSOCIATION, THURSDAY SOUGHT TO SOOTHE HER SOUL REFLECTION. SHE THOUGHT TO LOSE HER CAST COMPULSION, TO EXORCISE HER DEMON DIVERSION, THAT BLACK REFRACTION OF WHO SHE DID NOT KNOW, AND WOULD NOT AFFILIATE GIVEN ANY CHOICE. IT WAS THE PECULIAR ANGLE OF THE SUN THAT STRUCK HER SO DECIDUOUSLY, AND CAST ITS FICKLE RAYS ON EARTH, AND FOUND CURIOUS CURRENTS AROUND THURSDAY, THEREFORE GRANTING THE COSMIC BLINK TO THE INK OF BLACK AND BAD AT HER BACK. TOO SAD, THAT THURSDAY'S SHADOW WAS BAD, SO BAD. THURSDAY'S SHADOW WAS BAD.
STORY BY DAVE NOE
ART BY JOSH DECK
COLORS BY KEVIN HALTER

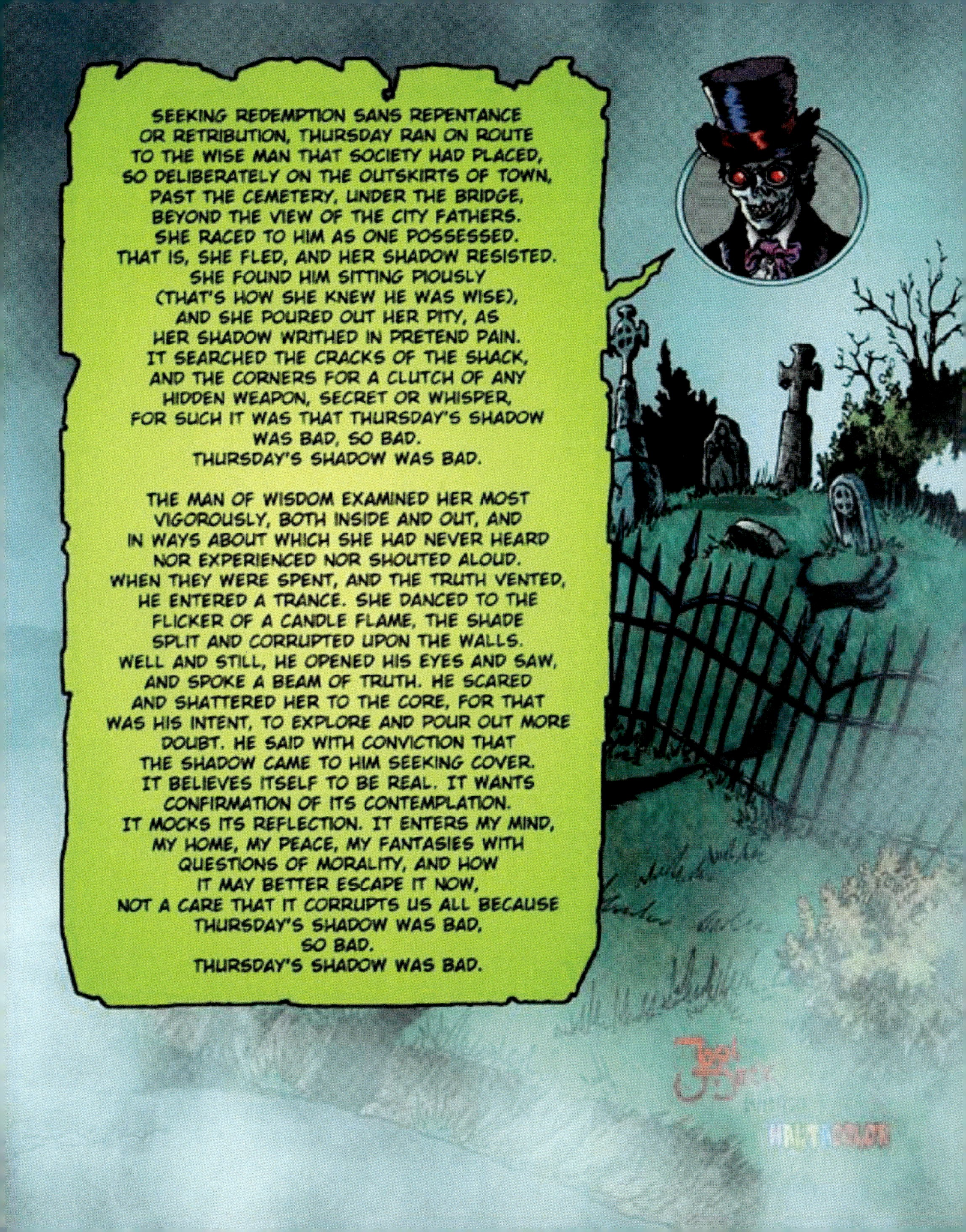
SEEKING REDEMPTION SANS REPENTANCE
OR RETRIBUTION, THURSDAY RAN ON ROUTE
TO THE WISE MAN THAT SOCIETY HAD PLACED,
SO DELIBERATELY ON THE OUTSKIRTS OF TOWN,
PAST THE CEMETERY, UNDER THE BRIDGE,
BEYOND THE VIEW OF THE CITY FATHERS.
SHE RACED TO HIM AS ONE POSSESSED.
THAT IS, SHE FLED, AND HER SHADOW RESISTED.
SHE FOUND HIM SITTING PIOUSLY
(THAT'S HOW SHE KNEW HE WAS WISE),
AND SHE POURED OUT HER PITY, AS
HER SHADOW WRITHED IN PRETEND PAIN.
IT SEARCHED THE CRACKS OF THE SHACK,
AND THE CORNERS FOR A CLUTCH OF ANY
HIDDEN WEAPON, SECRET OR WHISPER,
FOR SUCH IT WAS THAT THURSDAY'S SHADOW
WAS BAD, SO BAD.
THURSDAY'S SHADOW WAS BAD.

THE MAN OF WISDOM EXAMINED HER MOST
VIGOROUSLY, BOTH INSIDE AND OUT, AND
IN WAYS ABOUT WHICH SHE HAD NEVER HEARD
NOR EXPERIENCED NOR SHOUTED ALOUD.
WHEN THEY WERE SPENT, AND THE TRUTH VENTED,
HE ENTERED A TRANCE. SHE DANCED TO THE
FLICKER OF A CANDLE FLAME, THE SHADE
SPLIT AND CORRUPTED UPON THE WALLS.
WELL AND STILL, HE OPENED HIS EYES AND SAW,
AND SPOKE A BEAM OF TRUTH. HE SCARED
AND SHATTERED HER TO THE CORE, FOR THAT
WAS HIS INTENT, TO EXPLORE AND POUR OUT MORE
DOUBT. HE SAID WITH CONVICTION THAT
THE SHADOW CAME TO HIM SEEKING COVER.
IT BELIEVES ITSELF TO BE REAL. IT WANTS
CONFIRMATION OF ITS CONTEMPLATION.
IT MOCKS ITS REFLECTION. IT ENTERS MY MIND,
MY HOME, MY PEACE, MY FANTASIES WITH
QUESTIONS OF MORALITY, AND HOW
IT MAY BETTER ESCAPE IT NOW,
NOT A CARE THAT IT CORRUPTS US ALL BECAUSE
THURSDAY'S SHADOW WAS BAD,
SO BAD.
THURSDAY'S SHADOW WAS BAD.

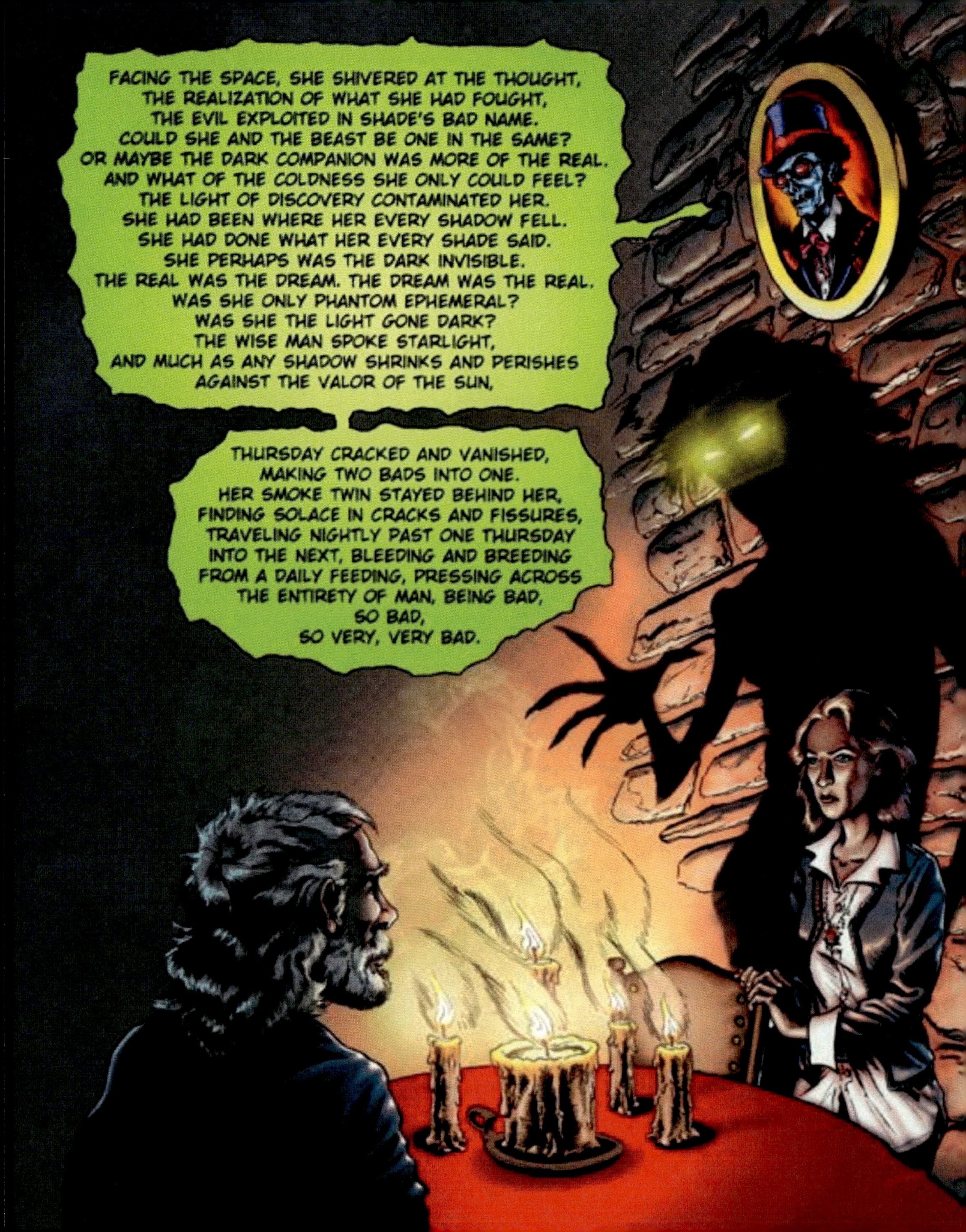
FACING THE SPACE, SHE SHIVERED AT THE THOUGHT,
THE REALIZATION OF WHAT SHE HAD FOUGHT,
THE EVIL EXPLOITED IN SHADE'S BAD NAME.
COULD SHE AND THE BEAST BE ONE IN THE SAME?
OR MAYBE THE DARK COMPANION WAS MORE OF THE REAL.
AND WHAT OF THE COLDNESS SHE ONLY COULD FEEL?
THE LIGHT OF DISCOVERY CONTAMINATED HER.
SHE HAD BEEN WHERE HER EVERY SHADOW FELL.
SHE HAD DONE WHAT HER EVERY SHADE SAID.
SHE PERHAPS WAS THE DARK INVISIBLE.
THE REAL WAS THE DREAM. THE DREAM WAS THE REAL.
WAS SHE ONLY PHANTOM EPHEMERAL?
WAS SHE THE LIGHT GONE DARK?
THE WISE MAN SPOKE STARLIGHT,
AND MUCH AS ANY SHADOW SHRINKS AND PERISHES
AGAINST THE VALOR OF THE SUN,
THURSDAY CRACKED AND VANISHED,
MAKING TWO BADS INTO ONE.
HER SMOKE TWIN STAYED BEHIND HER,
FINDING SOLACE IN CRACKS AND FISSURES,
TRAVELING NIGHTLY PAST ONE THURSDAY
INTO THE NEXT, BLEEDING AND BREEDING
FROM A DAILY FEEDING, PRESSING ACROSS
THE ENTIRETY OF MAN, BEING BAD,
SO BAD,
SO VERY, VERY BAD.

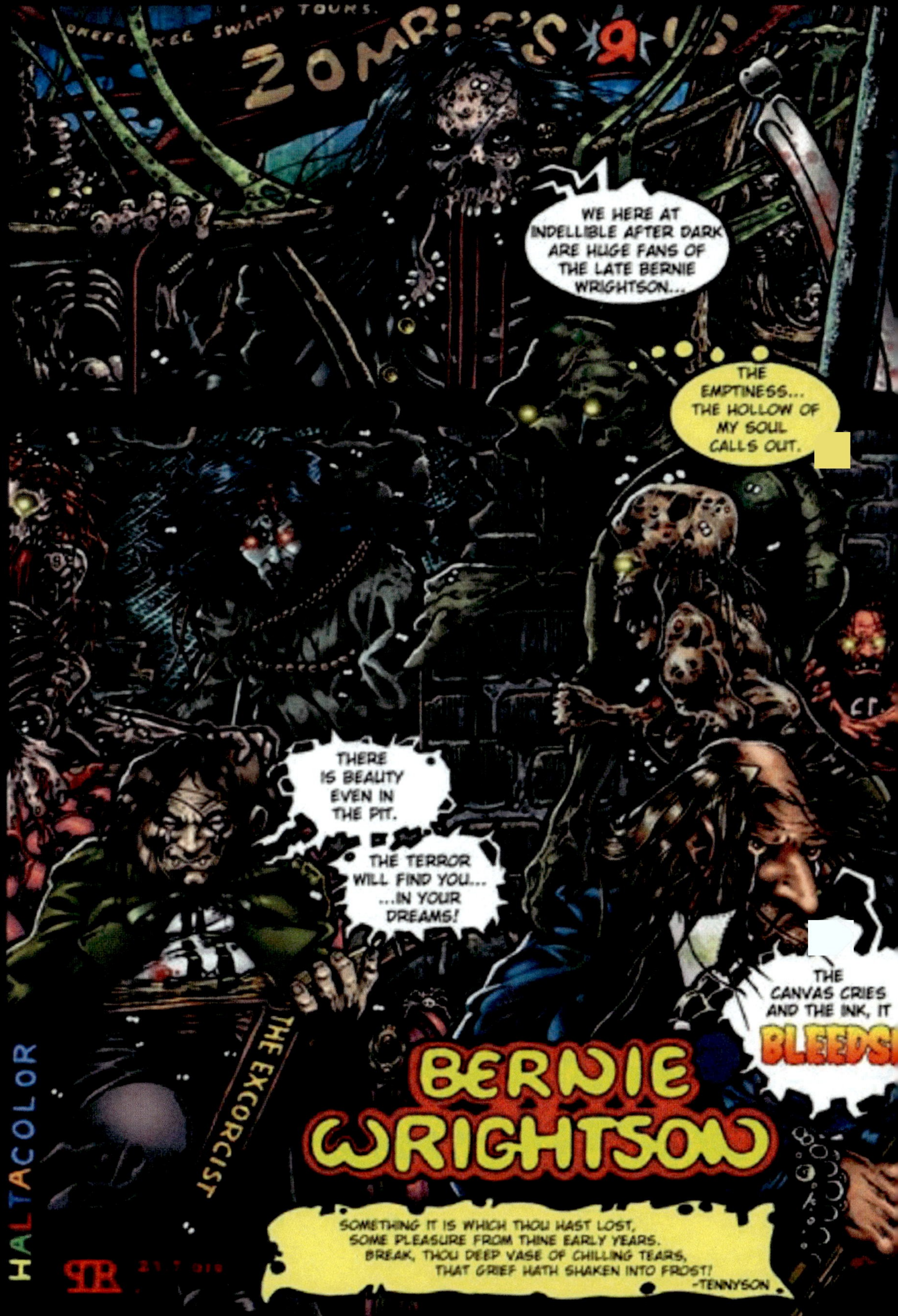
SWAMP TOURS.
WE HERE AT INDELLIBLE AFTER DARK ARE HUGE FANS OF THE LATE BERNIE WRIGHTSON...
THE EMPTINESS... THE HOLLOW OF MY SOUL CALLS OUT.
THERE IS BEAUTY EVEN IN THE PIT.
THE TERROR WILL FIND YOU... ...IN YOUR DREAMS!
THE CANVAS CRIES AND THE INK, IT
THE EXCORCIST
BERNIE WRIGHTSON
SOMETHING IT IS WHICH THOU HAST LOST,
SOME PLEASURE FROM THINE EARLY YEARS.
BREAK, THOU DEEP VASE OF CHILLING TEARS,
THAT GRIEF HATH SHAKEN INTO FROST!
-TENNYSON
HALTACOLOR

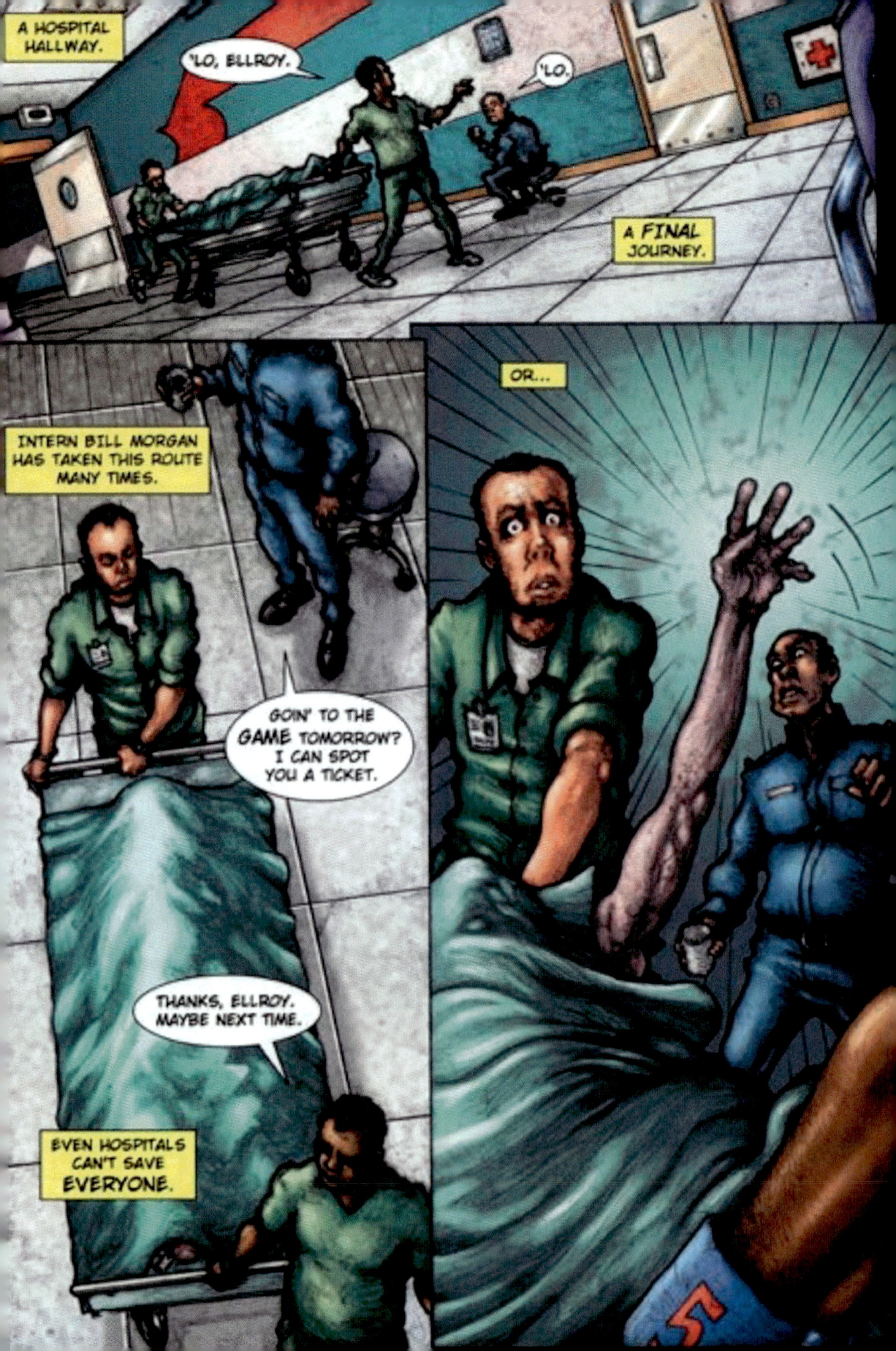
A HOSPITAL HALLWAY.
'LO, ELLROY.
'LO.
A FINAL JOURNEY.
INTERN BILL MORGAN HAS TAKEN THIS ROUTE MANY TIMES.
GOIN' TO THE GAME TOMORROW? I CAN SPOT YOU A TICKET.
THANKS, ELLROY. MAYBE NEXT TIME.
EVEN HOSPITALS CAN'T SAVE EVERYONE.
OR...

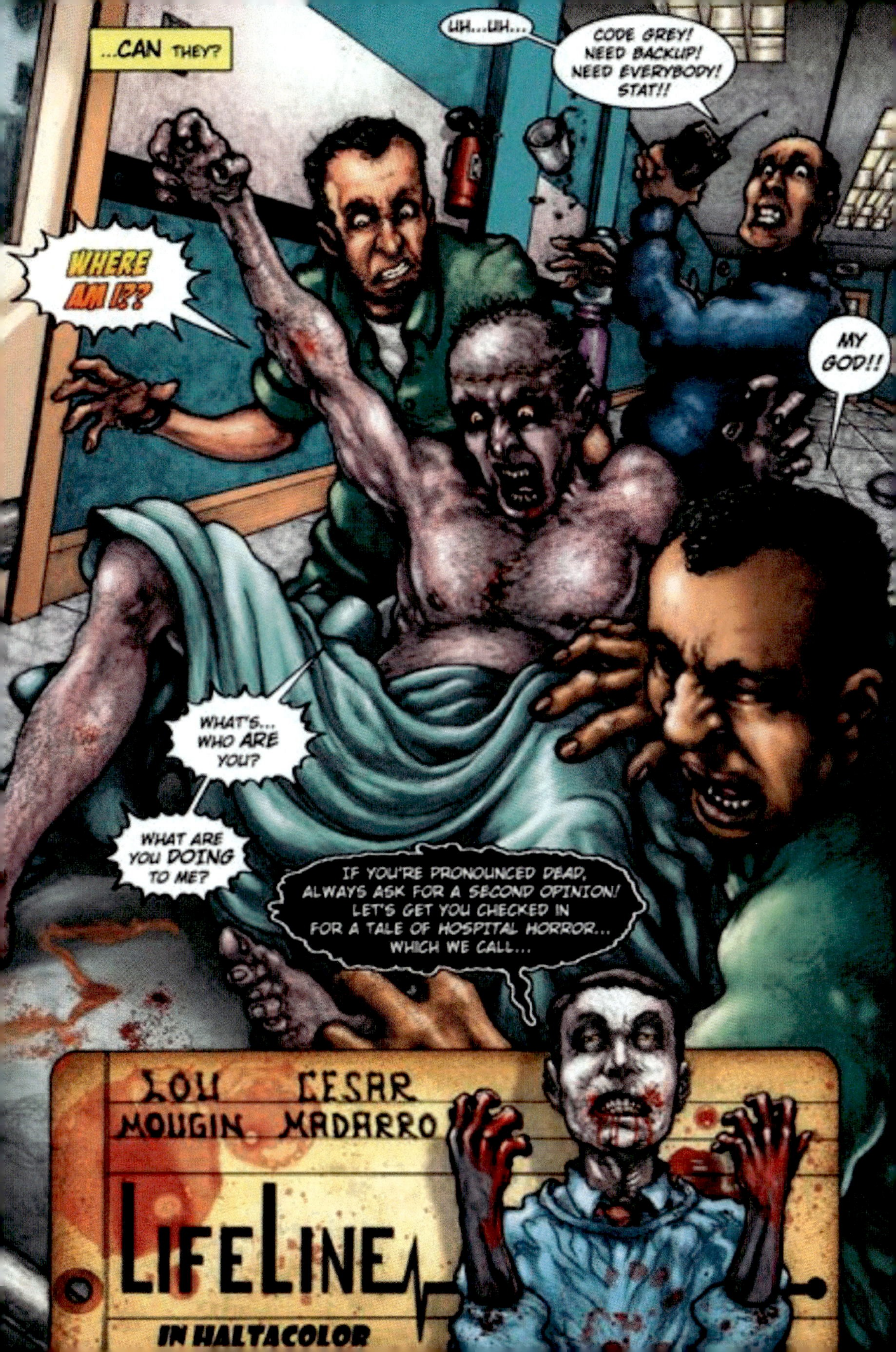
...CAN THEY?
UH...UH...
CODE GREY! NEED BACKUP! NEED EVERYBODY! STAT!!
WHERE AM I??
MY GOD!!
WHAT'S... WHO ARE YOU?
WHAT ARE YOU DOING TO ME?
IF YOU'RE PRONOUNCED DEAD, ALWAYS ASK FOR A SECOND OPINION! LET'S GET YOU CHECKED IN FOR A TALE OF HOSPITAL HORROR... WHICH WE CALL...
LOU MOUGIN
CESAR MADARRO
LIFELINE
IN HALTACOLOR

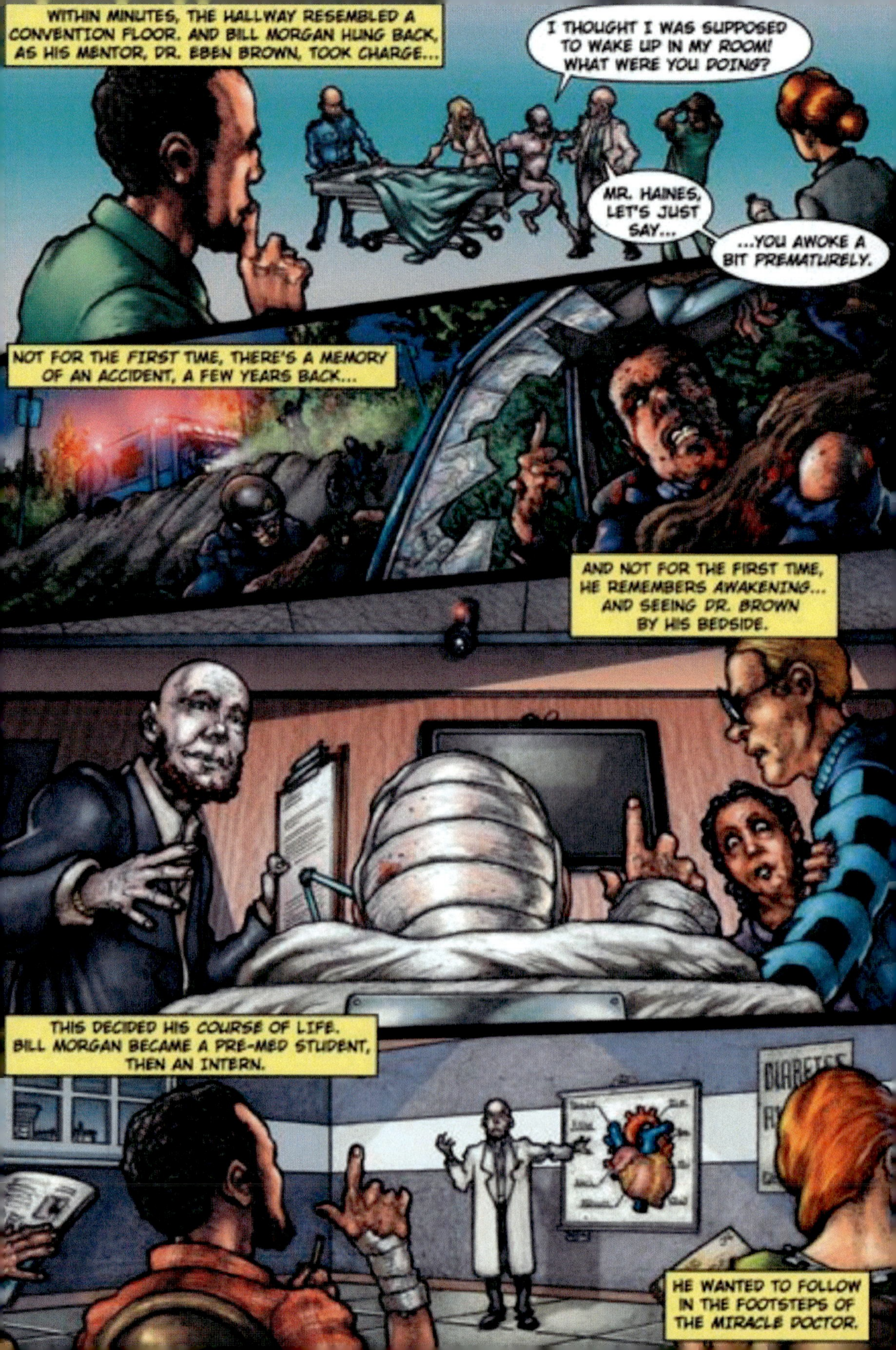
WITHIN MINUTES, THE HALLWAY RESEMBLED A CONVENTION FLOOR. AND BILL MORGAN HUNG BACK, AS HIS MENTOR, DR. EBEN BROWN, TOOK CHARGE...
I THOUGHT I WAS SUPPOSED TO WAKE UP IN MY ROOM! WHAT WERE YOU DOING?
MR. HAINES, LET'S JUST SAY...
...YOU AWOKE A BIT PREMATURELY.
NOT FOR THE FIRST TIME, THERE'S A MEMORY OF AN ACCIDENT, A FEW YEARS BACK...
AND NOT FOR THE FIRST TIME, HE REMEMBERS AWAKENING... AND SEEING DR. BROWN BY HIS BEDSIDE.
THIS DECIDED HIS COURSE OF LIFE. BILL MORGAN BECAME A PRE-MED STUDENT, THEN AN INTERN.
HE WANTED TO FOLLOW IN THE FOOTSTEPS OF THE MIRACLE DOCTOR.

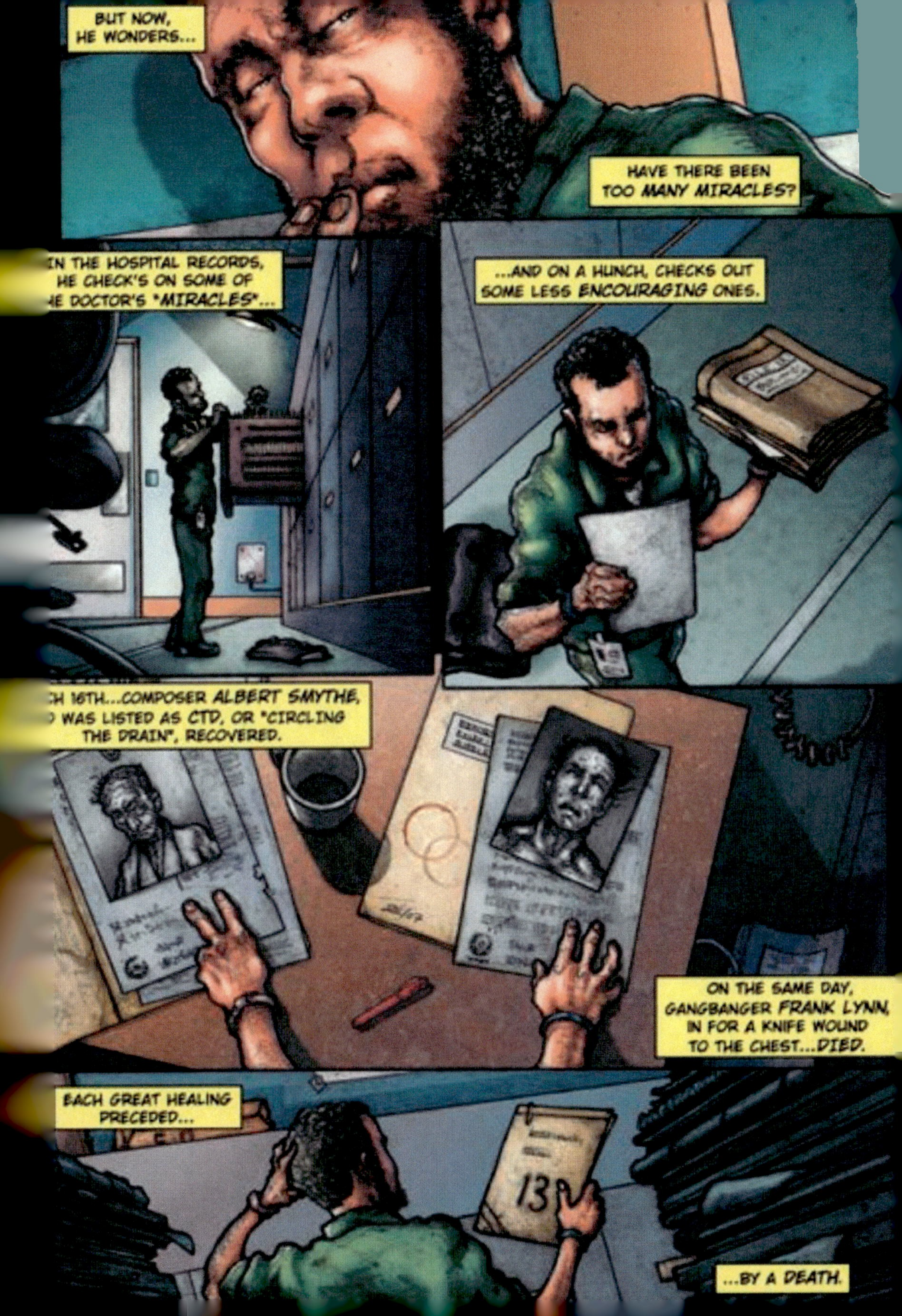

BUT NOW, HE WONDERS...
HAVE THERE BEEN TOO *MANY MIRACLES?*
IN THE HOSPITAL RECORDS, HE CHECK'S ON SOME OF HE DOCTOR'S "*MIRACLES*"...
...AND ON A HUNCH, CHECKS OUT SOME LESS *ENCOURAGING* ONES.
CH 16TH...COMPOSER *ALBERT SMYTHE,* WAS LISTED AS *CTD,* OR "CIRCLING THE DRAIN", RECOVERED.
ON THE SAME DAY, GANGBANGER *FRANK LYNN,* IN FOR A KNIFE WOUND TO THE CHEST...*DIED.*
EACH GREAT HEALING PRECEDED...
13
...BY A *DEATH.*

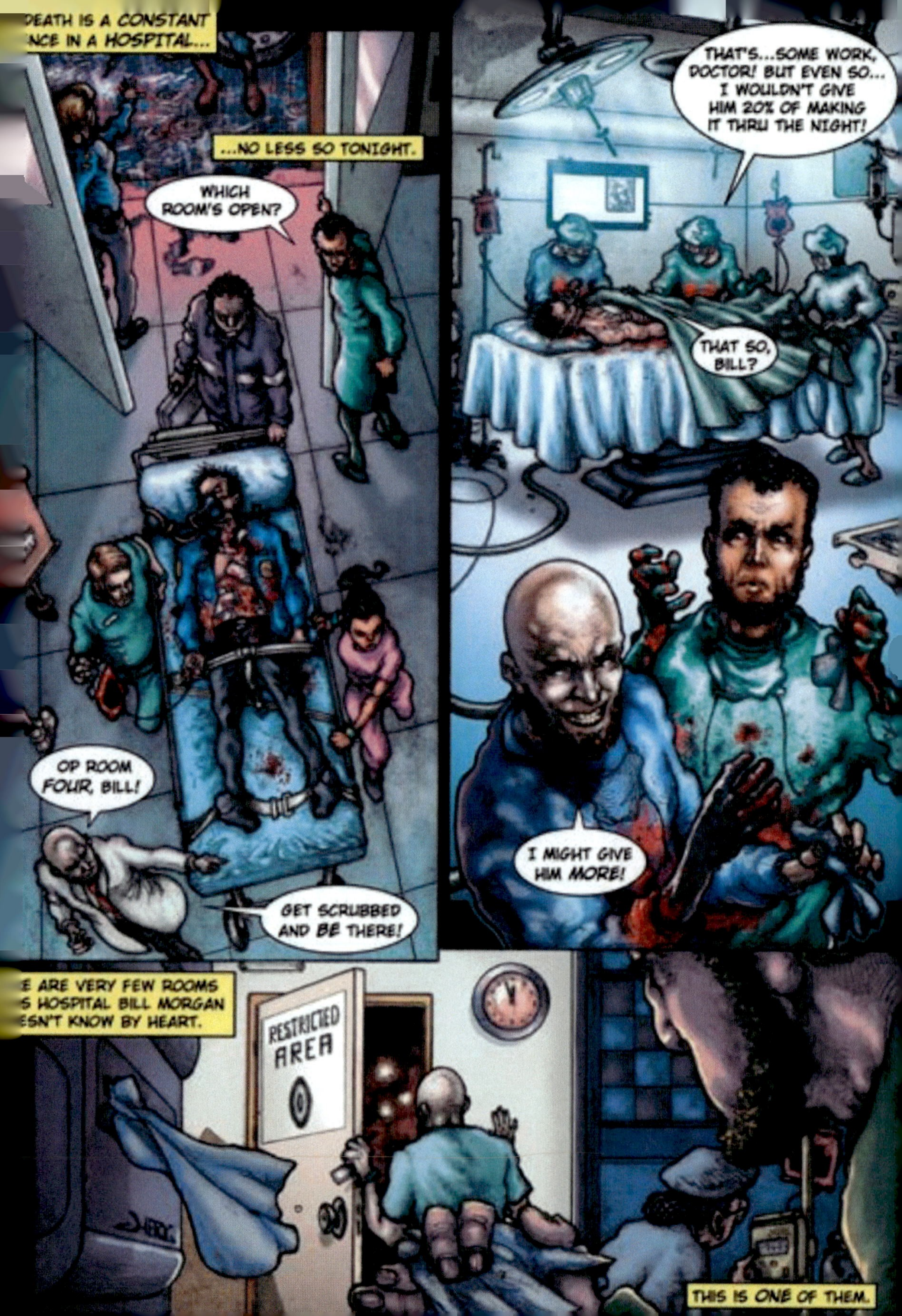
DEATH IS A CONSTANT
NCE IN A HOSPITAL...
...NO LESS SO TONIGHT.
WHICH ROOM'S OPEN?
OP ROOM FOUR, BILL!
GET SCRUBBED AND BE THERE!
THAT'S...SOME WORK, DOCTOR! BUT EVEN SO... I WOULDN'T GIVE HIM 20% OF MAKING IT THRU THE NIGHT!
THAT SO, BILL?
I MIGHT GIVE HIM MORE!
E ARE VERY FEW ROOMS
S HOSPITAL BILL MORGAN
ESN'T KNOW BY HEART.
RESTRICTED AREA
THIS IS ONE OF THEM.

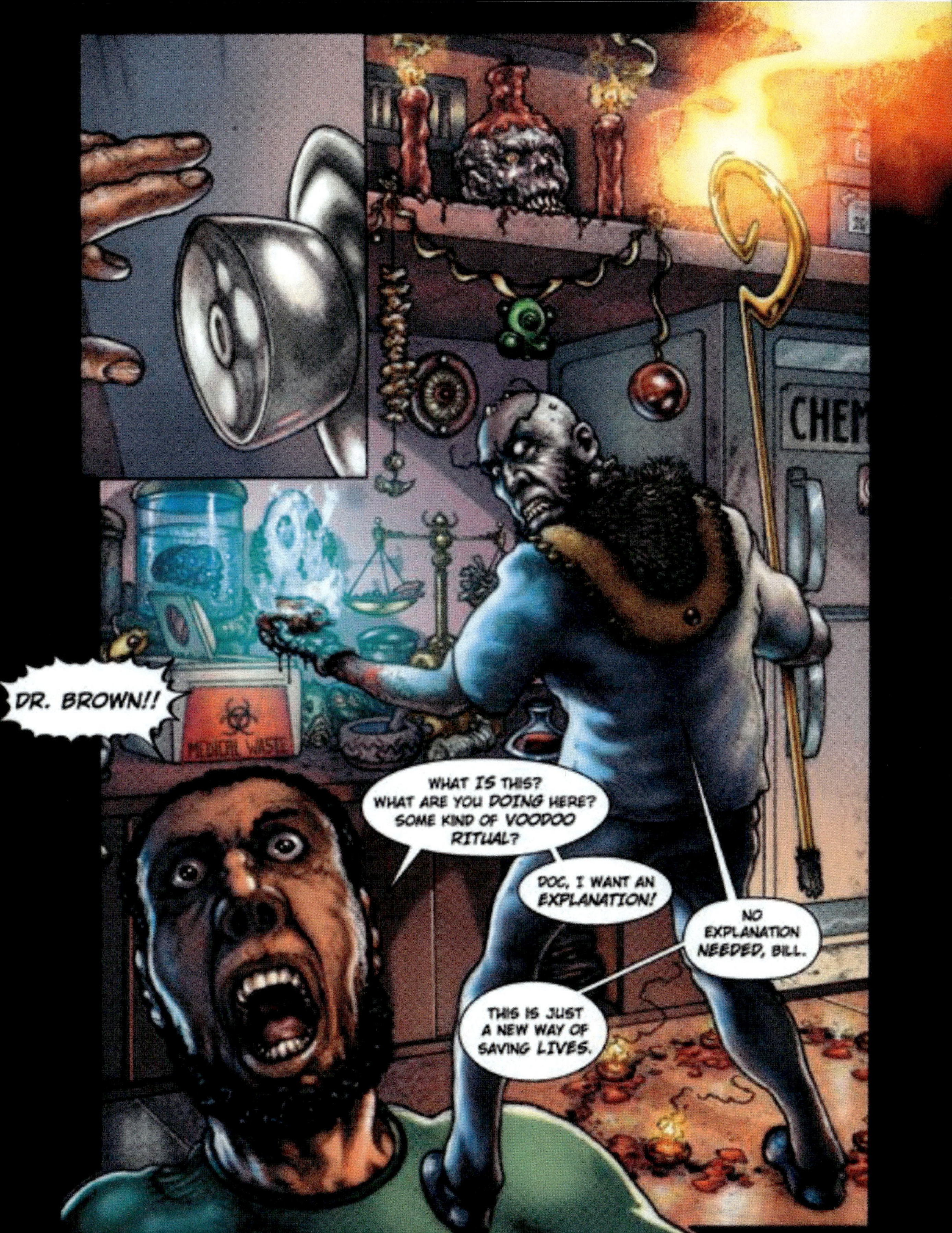
CHEM
MEDICAL WASTE
DR. BROWN!!
WHAT IS THIS? WHAT ARE YOU DOING HERE? SOME KIND OF VOODOO RITUAL?
DOC, I WANT AN EXPLANATION!
NO EXPLANATION NEEDED, BILL.
THIS IS JUST A NEW WAY OF SAVING LIVES.

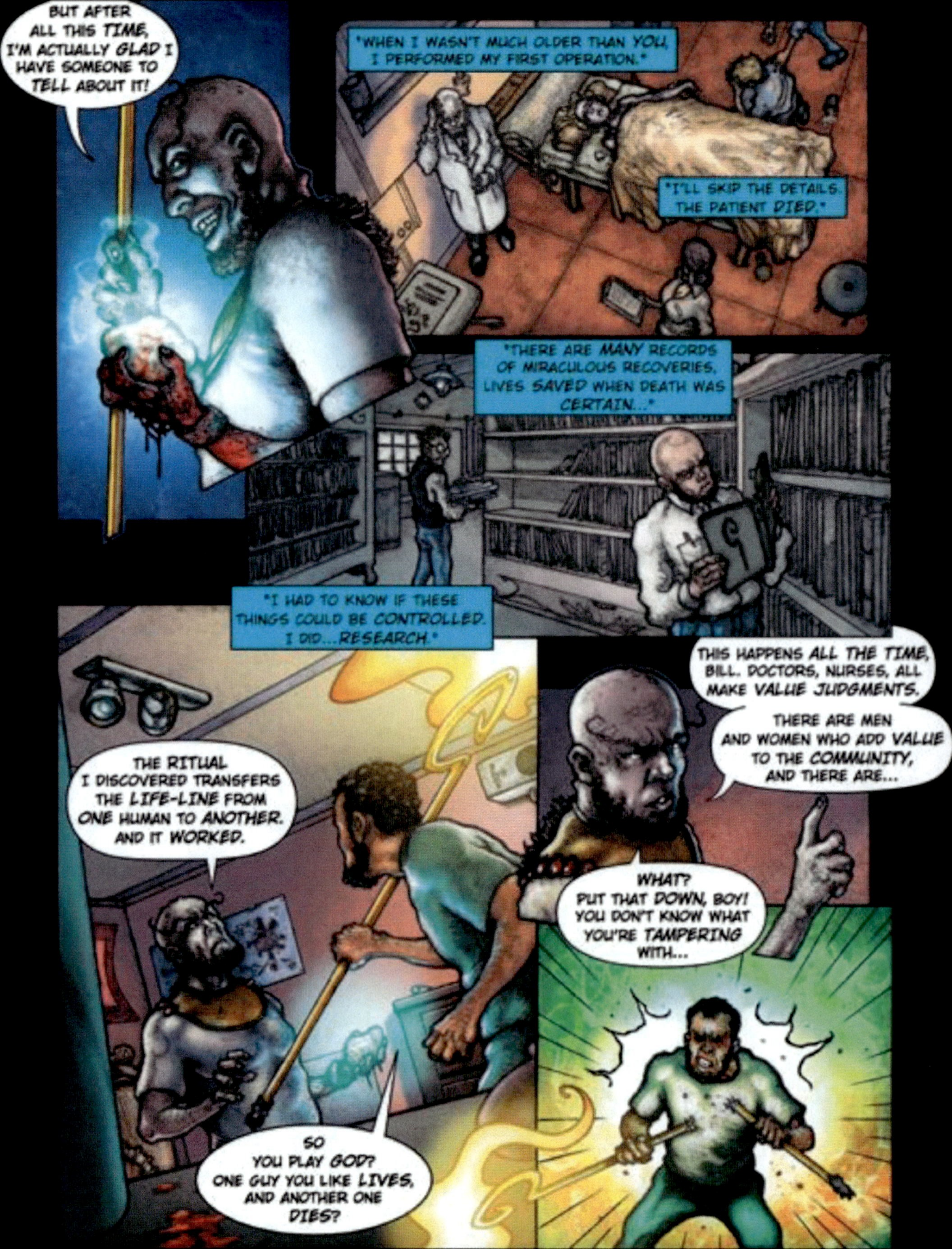
BUT AFTER ALL THIS TIME, I'M ACTUALLY GLAD I HAVE SOMEONE TO TELL ABOUT IT!
"WHEN I WASN'T MUCH OLDER THAN YOU, I PERFORMED MY FIRST OPERATION."
"I'LL SKIP THE DETAILS. THE PATIENT DIED."
"THERE ARE MANY RECORDS OF MIRACULOUS RECOVERIES, LIVES SAVED WHEN DEATH WAS CERTAIN..."
"I HAD TO KNOW IF THESE THINGS COULD BE CONTROLLED. I DID...RESEARCH."
THE RITUAL I DISCOVERED TRANSFERS THE LIFE-LINE FROM ONE HUMAN TO ANOTHER. AND IT WORKED.
SO YOU PLAY GOD? ONE GUY YOU LIKE LIVES, AND ANOTHER ONE DIES?
THIS HAPPENS ALL THE TIME, BILL. DOCTORS, NURSES, ALL MAKE VALUE JUDGMENTS.
THERE ARE MEN AND WOMEN WHO ADD VALUE TO THE COMMUNITY, AND THERE ARE...
WHAT? PUT THAT DOWN, BOY! YOU DON'T KNOW WHAT YOU'RE TAMPERING WITH...

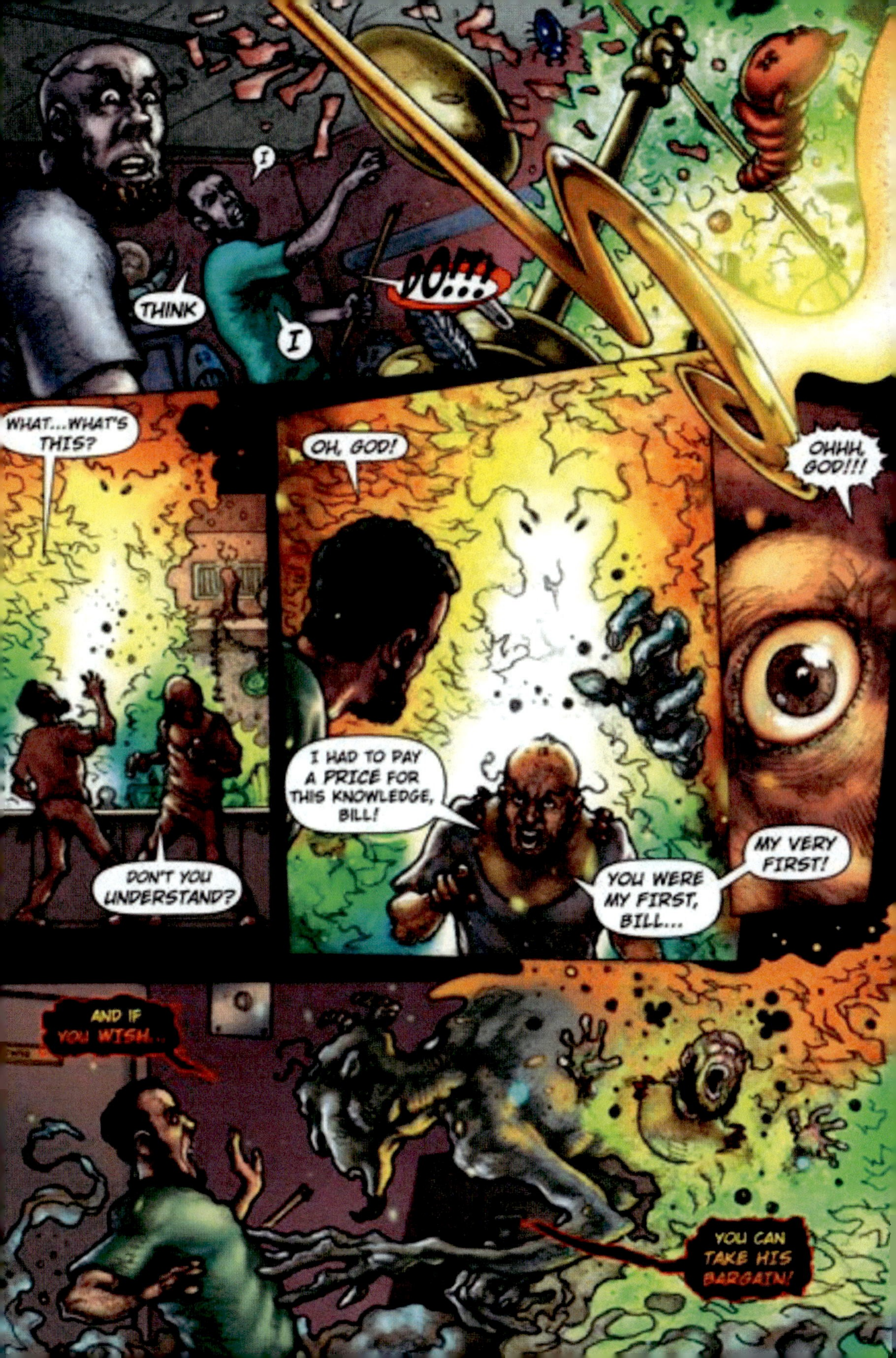
I
THINK
I
DO!!!
WHAT...WHAT'S THIS?
DON'T YOU UNDERSTAND?
OH, GOD!
I HAD TO PAY A PRICE FOR THIS KNOWLEDGE, BILL!
YOU WERE MY FIRST, BILL...
OHHH, GOD!!!
MY VERY FIRST!
AND IF YOU WISH...
YOU CAN TAKE HIS BARGAIN!

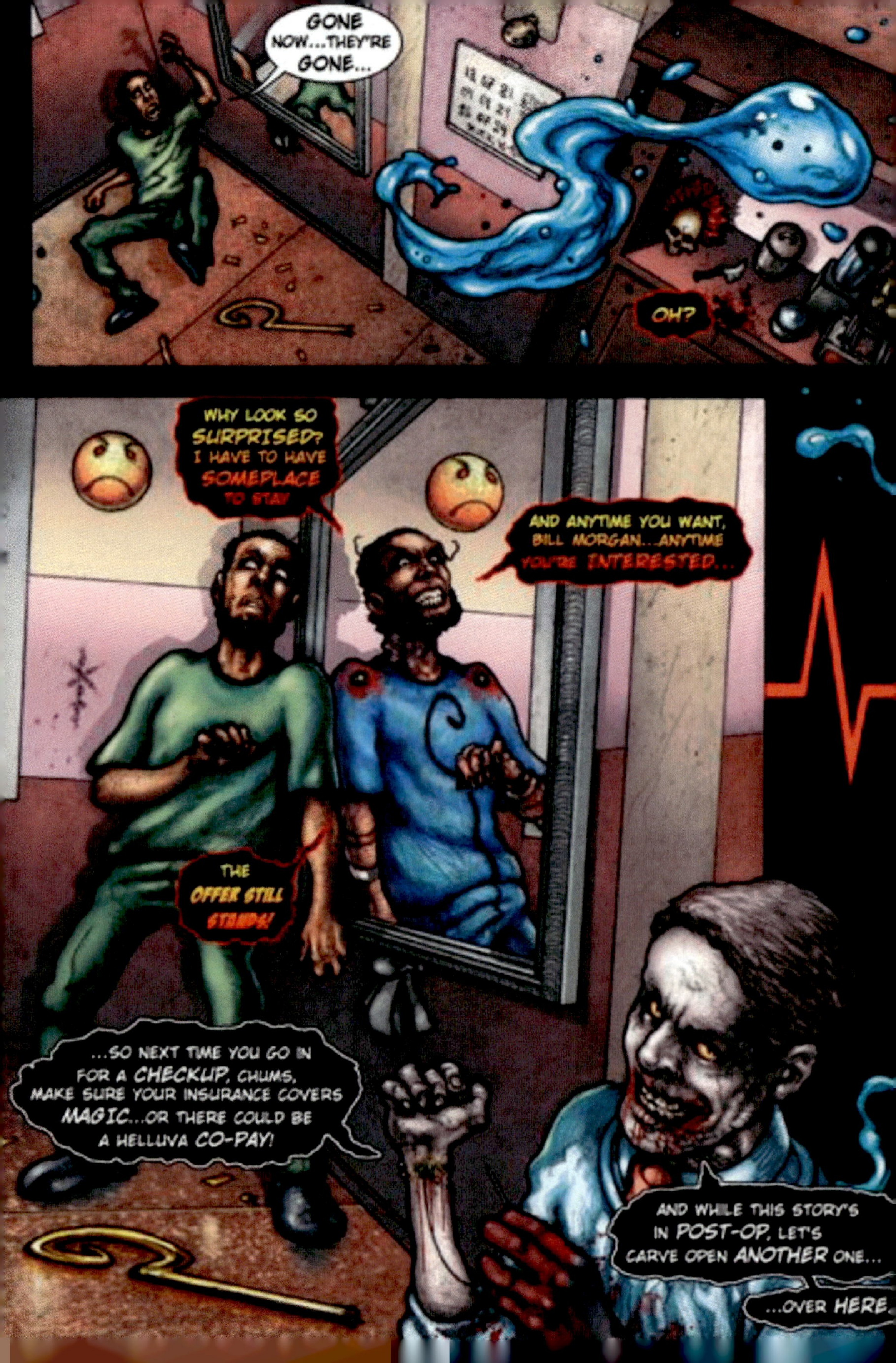
GONE NOW...THEY'RE GONE...
OH?
WHY LOOK SO SURPRISED? I HAVE TO HAVE SOMEPLACE TO STAY
AND ANYTIME YOU WANT, BILL MORGAN...ANYTIME YOU'RE INTERESTED...
THE OFFER STILL STANDS!
...SO NEXT TIME YOU GO IN FOR A CHECKUP, CHUMS, MAKE SURE YOUR INSURANCE COVERS MAGIC...OR THERE COULD BE A HELLUVA CO-PAY!
AND WHILE THIS STORY'S IN POST-OP, LET'S CARVE OPEN ANOTHER ONE...
...OVER HERE.

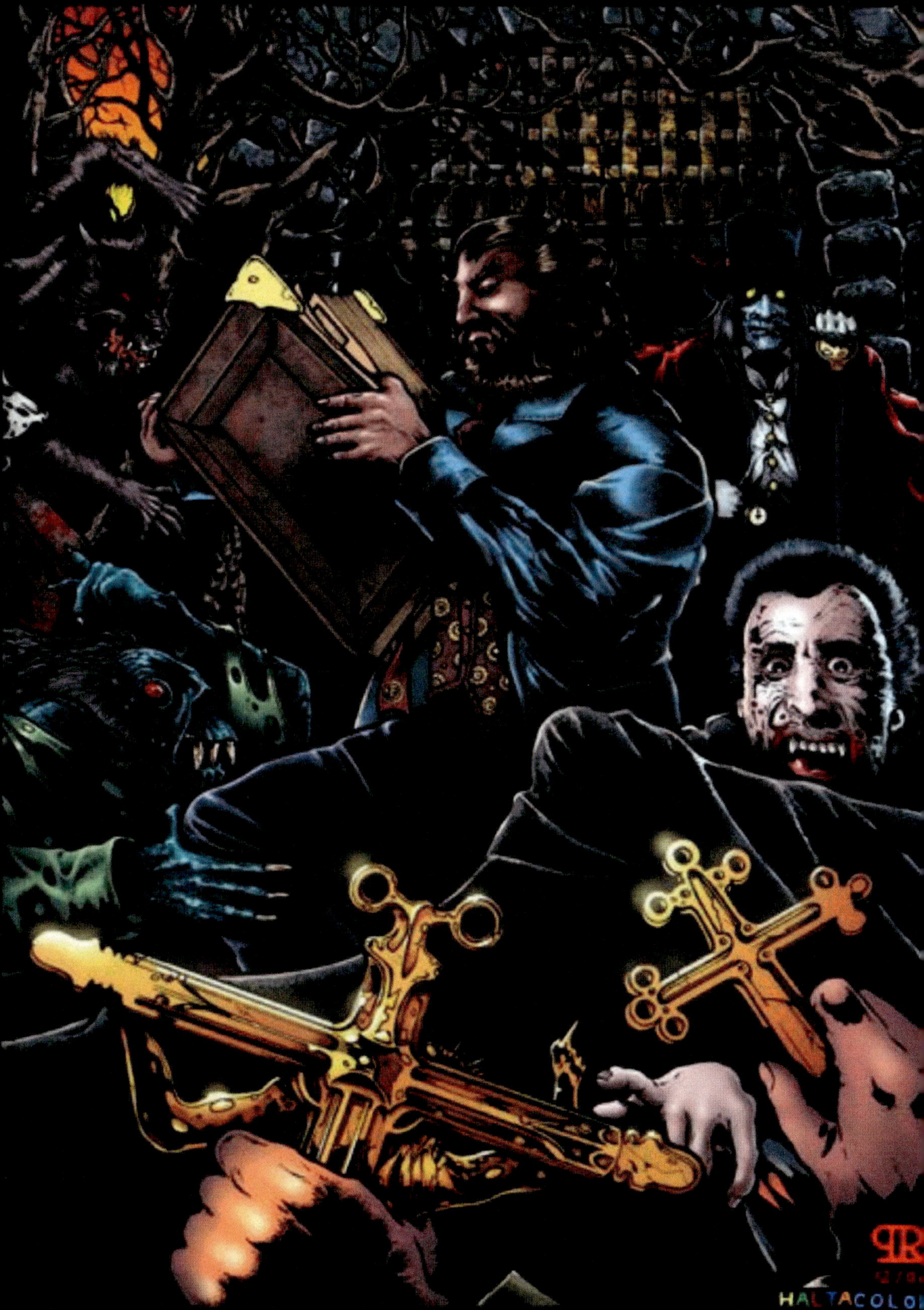

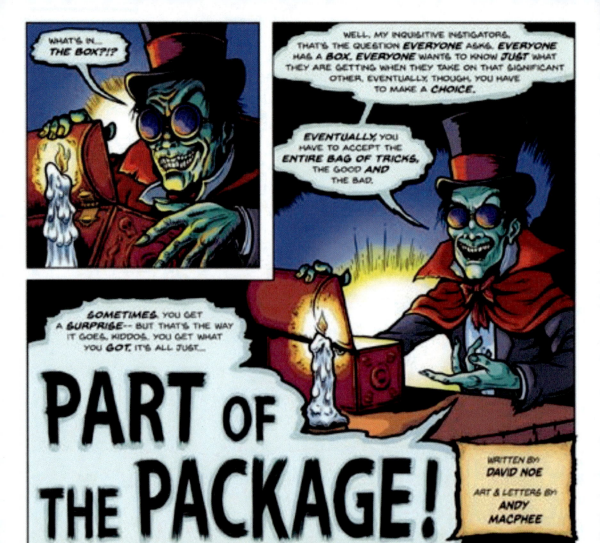

WHAT'S IN... *THE BOX?!?*

WELL, MY INQUISITIVE INSTIGATORS, THAT'S THE QUESTION *EVERYONE* ASKS. *EVERYONE* HAS A *BOX. EVERYONE* WANTS TO KNOW *JUST* WHAT THEY ARE GETTING WHEN THEY TAKE ON THAT SIGNIFICANT OTHER. EVENTUALLY, THOUGH, YOU HAVE TO MAKE A *CHOICE.*

EVENTUALLY, YOU HAVE TO ACCEPT THE *ENTIRE BAG OF TRICKS,* THE GOOD *AND* THE BAD.

SOMETIMES, YOU GET A *SURPRISE--* BUT THAT'S THE WAY IT GOES, KIDDOS. YOU GET WHAT YOU *GOT.* IT'S ALL JUST...

PART OF THE PACKAGE!

WRITTEN BY: **DAVID NOE**

ART & LETTERS BY: **ANDY MACPHEE**

MY NAME IS *SIRENNA STAR.* YOU MAY HAVE HEARD OF ME. I WAS A MINOR CELEBRITY IN THE EARLY '50S ON THE RADIO, AND EVEN IN SOME MOTION PICTURES. THIS IS A PICTURE OF ME AT MY LAST PERFORMANCE AT THE W.H.O. RADIO STUDIO.

BUT I GAVE THAT ALL UP WHEN MY VINNIE CAME BACK FROM THE WAR. NOW IT WAS BACK TO BEING *"SIRENNA BOGDONAVICH,"* THE LUCKIEST HOUSEWIFE THIS SIDE OF CHICAGO.

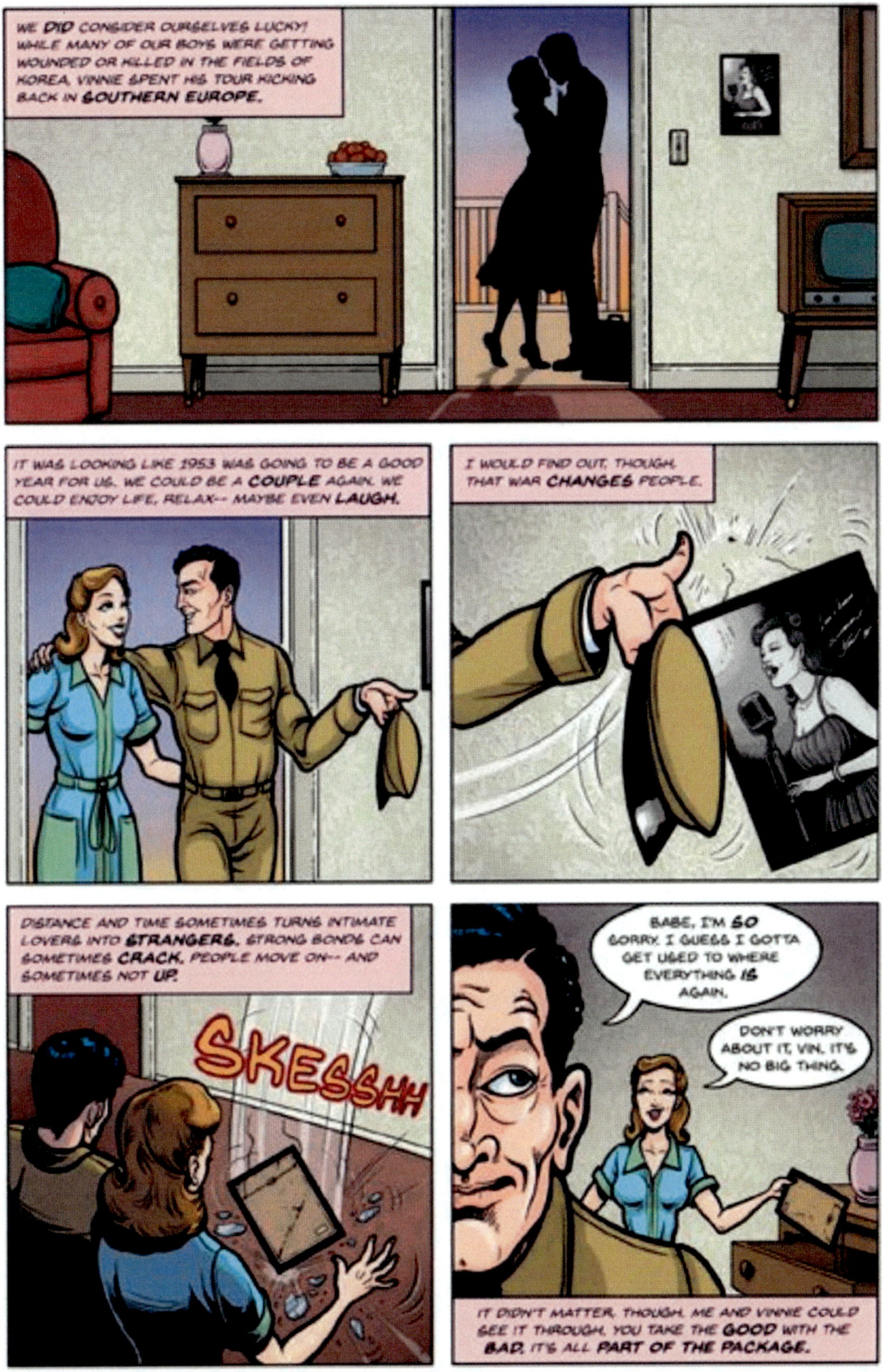
WE DID CONSIDER OURSELVES LUCKY! WHILE MANY OF OUR BOYS WERE GETTING WOUNDED OR KILLED IN THE FIELDS OF KOREA, VINNIE SPENT HIS TOUR KICKING BACK IN SOUTHERN EUROPE.
IT WAS LOOKING LIKE 1953 WAS GOING TO BE A GOOD YEAR FOR US. WE COULD BE A COUPLE AGAIN. WE COULD ENJOY LIFE, RELAX-- MAYBE EVEN LAUGH.
I WOULD FIND OUT, THOUGH, THAT WAR CHANGES PEOPLE.
DISTANCE AND TIME SOMETIMES TURNS INTIMATE LOVERS INTO STRANGERS. STRONG BONDS CAN SOMETIMES CRACK. PEOPLE MOVE ON-- AND SOMETIMES NOT UP.
SKESSHH
BABE, I'M SO SORRY. I GUESS I GOTTA GET USED TO WHERE EVERYTHING IS AGAIN.
DON'T WORRY ABOUT IT, VIN. IT'S NO BIG THING.
IT DIDN'T MATTER, THOUGH. ME AND VINNIE COULD SEE IT THROUGH. YOU TAKE THE GOOD WITH THE BAD. IT'S ALL PART OF THE PACKAGE.

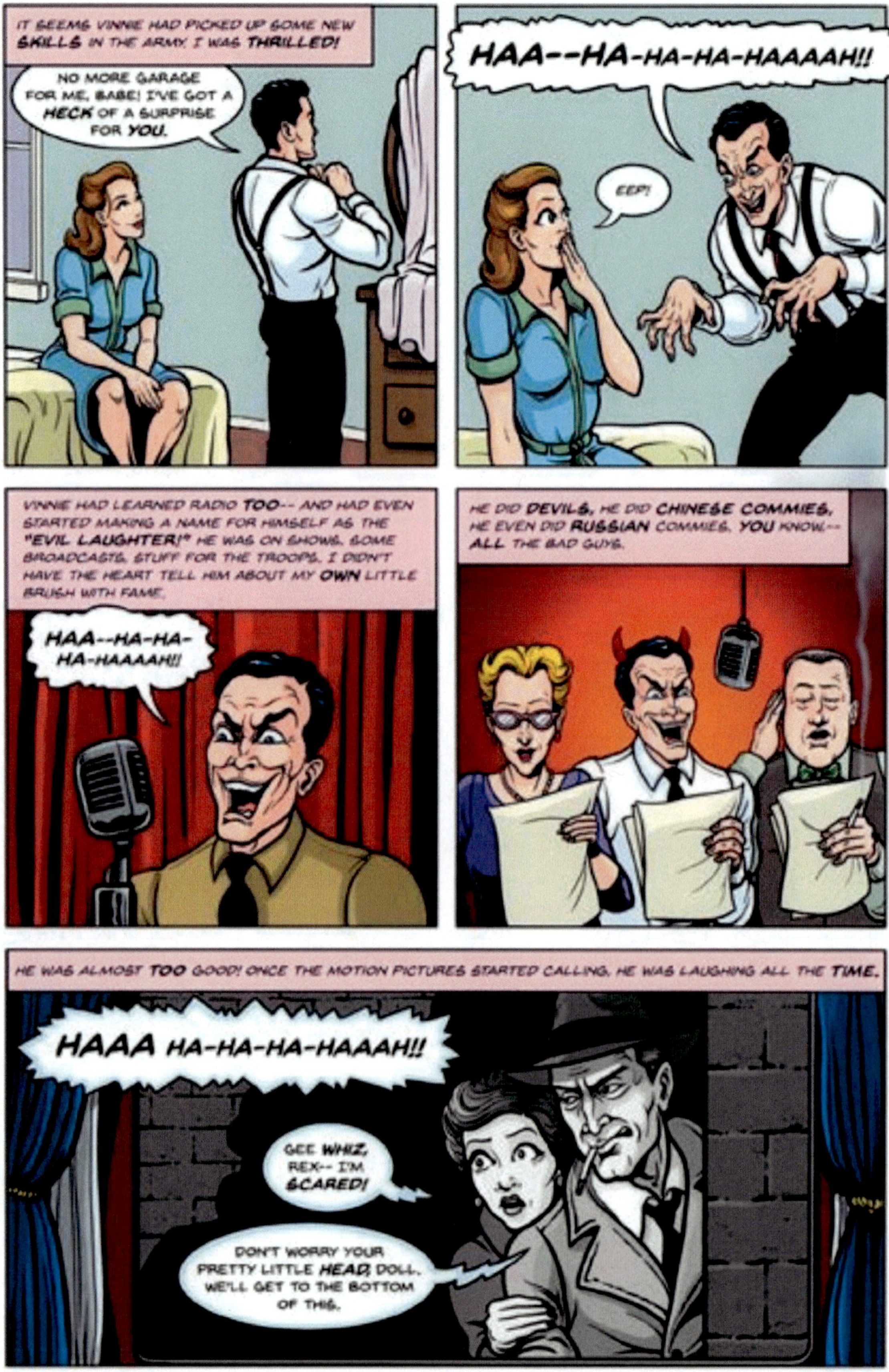
IT SEEMS VINNIE HAD PICKED UP SOME NEW SKILLS IN THE ARMY. I WAS THRILLED!
NO MORE GARAGE FOR ME, BABE! I'VE GOT A HECK OF A SURPRISE FOR YOU.
HAA--HA-HA-HA-HAAAAH!!
EEP!
VINNIE HAD LEARNED RADIO TOO-- AND HAD EVEN STARTED MAKING A NAME FOR HIMSELF AS THE "EVIL LAUGHTER!" HE WAS ON SHOWS, SOME BROADCASTS, STUFF FOR THE TROOPS. I DIDN'T HAVE THE HEART TELL HIM ABOUT MY OWN LITTLE BRUSH WITH FAME.
HAA--HA-HA-HA-HAAAAH!!
HE DID DEVILS, HE DID CHINESE COMMIES, HE EVEN DID RUSSIAN COMMIES. YOU KNOW-- ALL THE BAD GUYS.
HE WAS ALMOST TOO GOOD! ONCE THE MOTION PICTURES STARTED CALLING, HE WAS LAUGHING ALL THE TIME.
HAAA HA-HA-HA-HAAAH!!
GEE WHIZ, REX-- I'M SCARED!
DON'T WORRY YOUR PRETTY LITTLE HEAD, DOLL. WE'LL GET TO THE BOTTOM OF THIS.

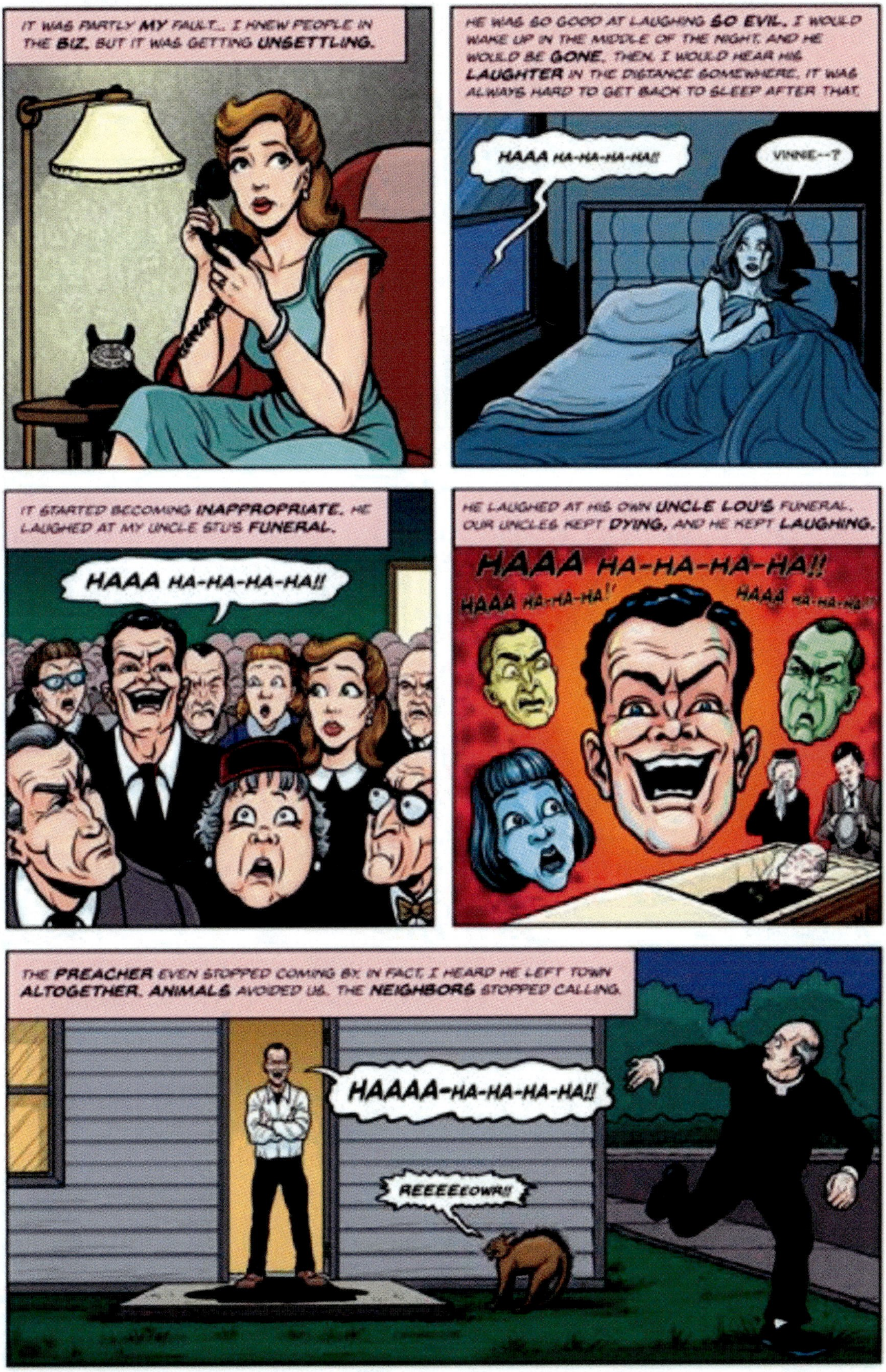
IT WAS PARTLY MY FAULT... I KNEW PEOPLE IN THE BIZ. BUT IT WAS GETTING UNSETTLING.
HE WAS SO GOOD AT LAUGHING SO EVIL. I WOULD WAKE UP IN THE MIDDLE OF THE NIGHT, AND HE WOULD BE GONE. THEN, I WOULD HEAR HIS LAUGHTER IN THE DISTANCE SOMEWHERE. IT WAS ALWAYS HARD TO GET BACK TO SLEEP AFTER THAT.
HAAA HA-HA-HA-HA!!
VINNIE--?
IT STARTED BECOMING INAPPROPRIATE. HE LAUGHED AT MY UNCLE STU'S FUNERAL.
HAAA HA-HA-HA-HA!!
HE LAUGHED AT HIS OWN UNCLE LOU'S FUNERAL. OUR UNCLES KEPT DYING, AND HE KEPT LAUGHING.
HAAA HA-HA-HA-HA!!
HAAA HA-HA-HA!!
HAAA HA-HA-HA!!
THE PREACHER EVEN STOPPED COMING BY. IN FACT, I HEARD HE LEFT TOWN ALTOGETHER. ANIMALS AVOIDED US. THE NEIGHBORS STOPPED CALLING.
HAAAA-HA-HA-HA-HA!!
REEEEEOWR!!

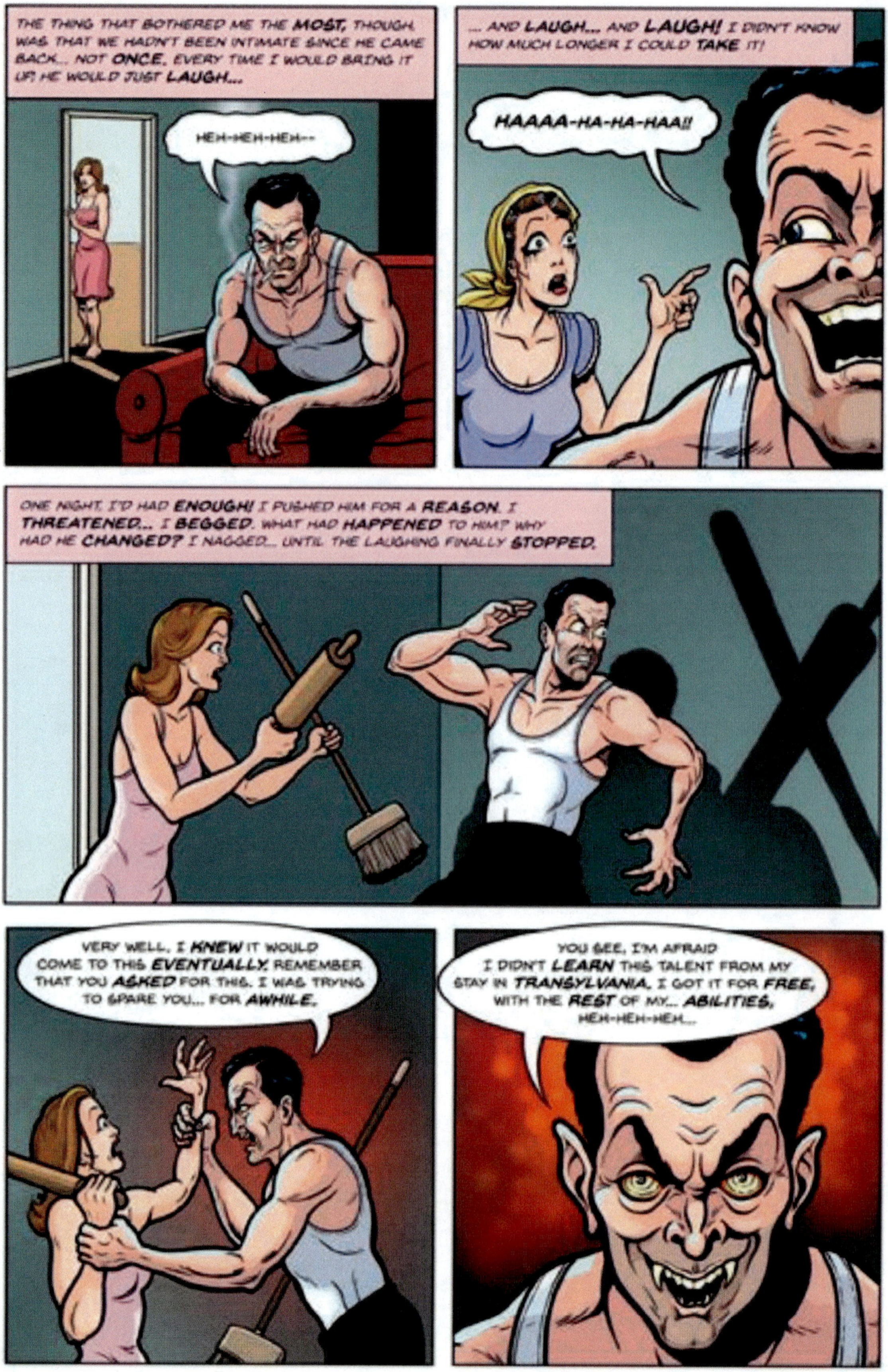
THE THING THAT BOTHERED ME THE MOST, THOUGH, WAS THAT WE HADN'T BEEN INTIMATE SINCE HE CAME BACK... NOT ONCE. EVERY TIME I WOULD BRING IT UP, HE WOULD JUST LAUGH...
HEH-HEH-HEH--
... AND LAUGH... AND LAUGH! I DIDN'T KNOW HOW MUCH LONGER I COULD TAKE IT!
HAAAA-HA-HA-HAA!!
ONE NIGHT, I'D HAD ENOUGH! I PUSHED HIM FOR A REASON. I THREATENED... I BEGGED. WHAT HAD HAPPENED TO HIM? WHY HAD HE CHANGED? I NAGGED... UNTIL THE LAUGHING FINALLY STOPPED.
VERY WELL, I KNEW IT WOULD COME TO THIS EVENTUALLY. REMEMBER THAT YOU ASKED FOR THIS. I WAS TRYING TO SPARE YOU... FOR AWHILE.
YOU SEE, I'M AFRAID I DIDN'T LEARN THIS TALENT FROM MY STAY IN TRANSYLVANIA. I GOT IT FOR FREE, WITH THE REST OF MY... ABILITIES. HEH-HEH-HEH...

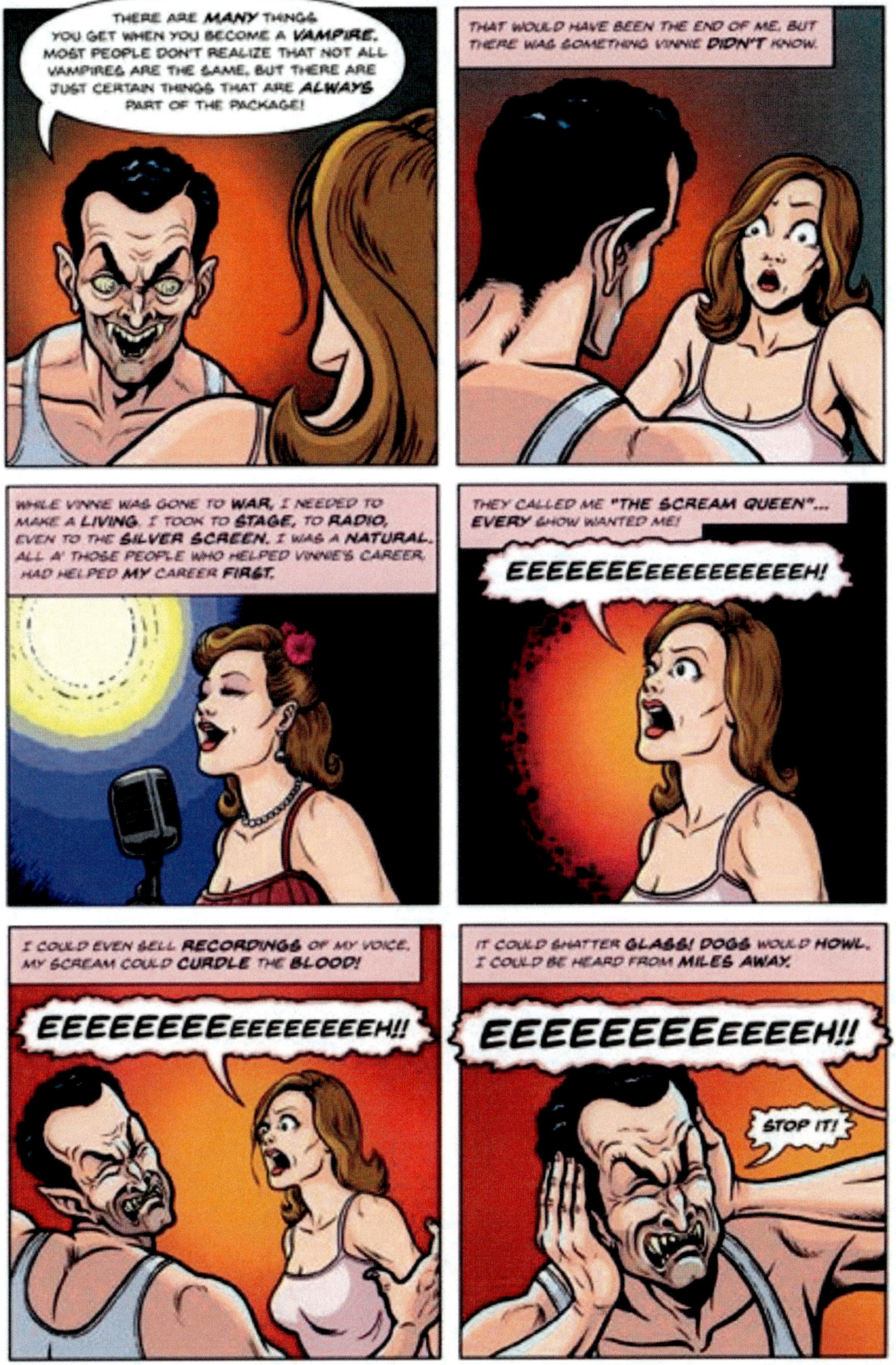
THERE ARE MANY THINGS YOU GET WHEN YOU BECOME A VAMPIRE. MOST PEOPLE DON'T REALIZE THAT NOT ALL VAMPIRES ARE THE SAME, BUT THERE ARE JUST CERTAIN THINGS THAT ARE ALWAYS PART OF THE PACKAGE!
THAT WOULD HAVE BEEN THE END OF ME, BUT THERE WAS SOMETHING VINNIE DIDN'T KNOW.
WHILE VINNIE WAS GONE TO WAR, I NEEDED TO MAKE A LIVING. I TOOK TO STAGE, TO RADIO, EVEN TO THE SILVER SCREEN. I WAS A NATURAL. ALL A' THOSE PEOPLE WHO HELPED VINNIE'S CAREER, HAD HELPED MY CAREER FIRST.
THEY CALLED ME "THE SCREAM QUEEN"... EVERY SHOW WANTED ME!
EEEEEEEEEEEEEEEEEH!
I COULD EVEN SELL RECORDINGS OF MY VOICE. MY SCREAM COULD CURDLE THE BLOOD!
EEEEEEEEEEEEEEEEEH!!
IT COULD SHATTER GLASS! DOGS WOULD HOWL. I COULD BE HEARD FROM MILES AWAY.
EEEEEEEEEEEEEH!!
STOP IT!

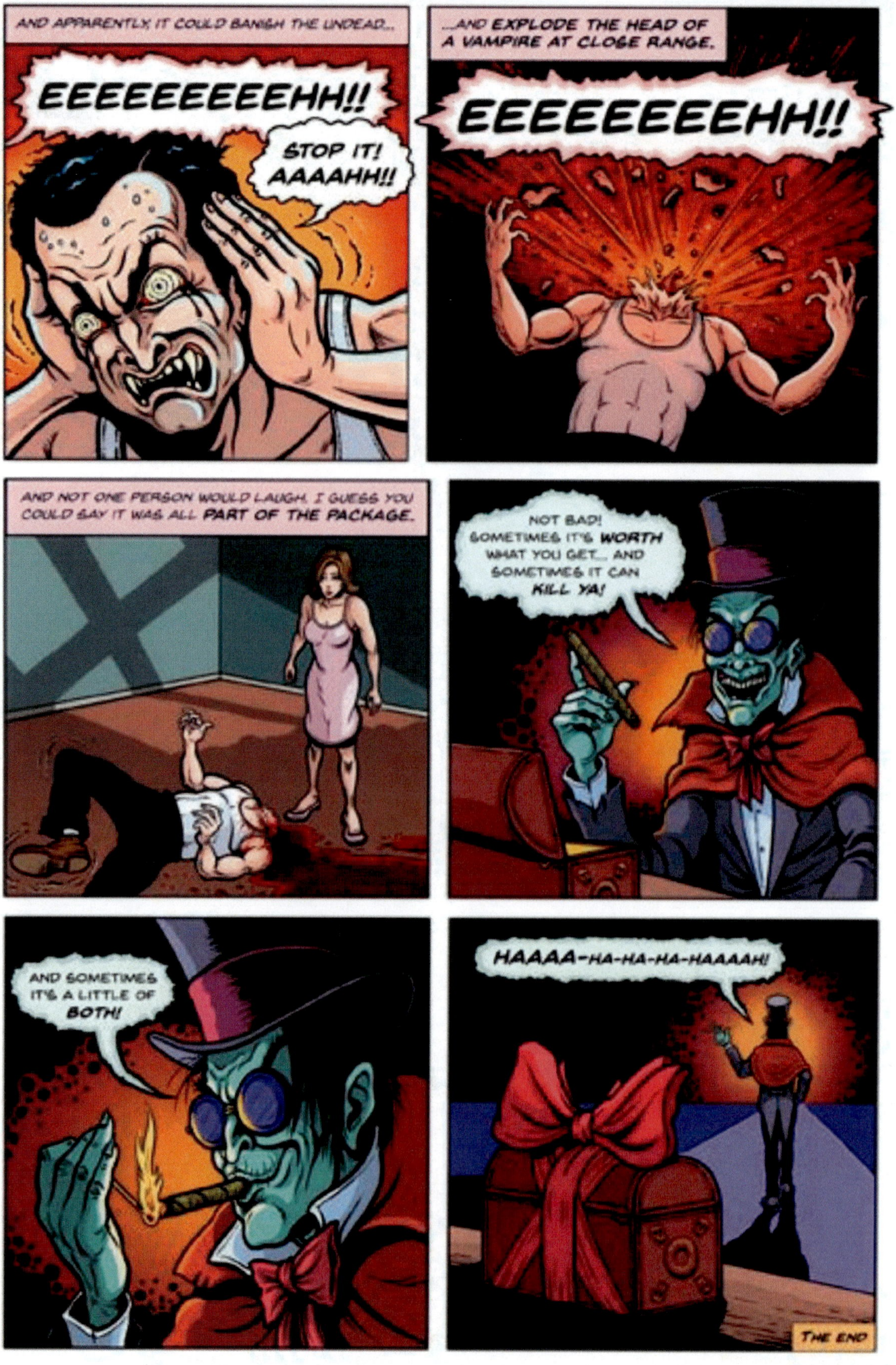
AND APPARENTLY, IT COULD BANISH THE UNDEAD...
EEEEEEEEEEHH!!
STOP IT! AAAAHH!!
...AND EXPLODE THE HEAD OF A VAMPIRE AT CLOSE RANGE.
EEEEEEEEEEHH!!
AND NOT ONE PERSON WOULD LAUGH. I GUESS YOU COULD SAY IT WAS ALL PART OF THE PACKAGE.
NOT BAD! SOMETIMES IT'S WORTH WHAT YOU GET... AND SOMETIMES IT CAN KILL YA!
AND SOMETIMES IT'S A LITTLE OF BOTH!
HAAAA-HA-HA-HA-HAAAAH!
THE END

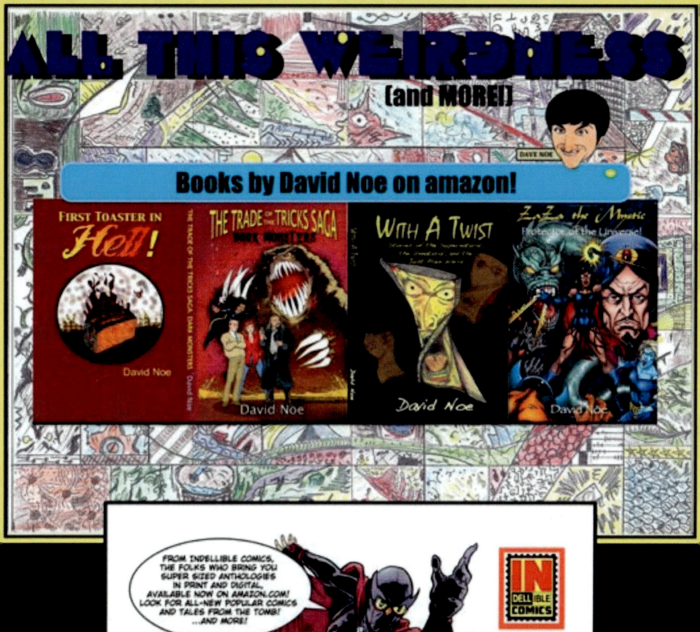

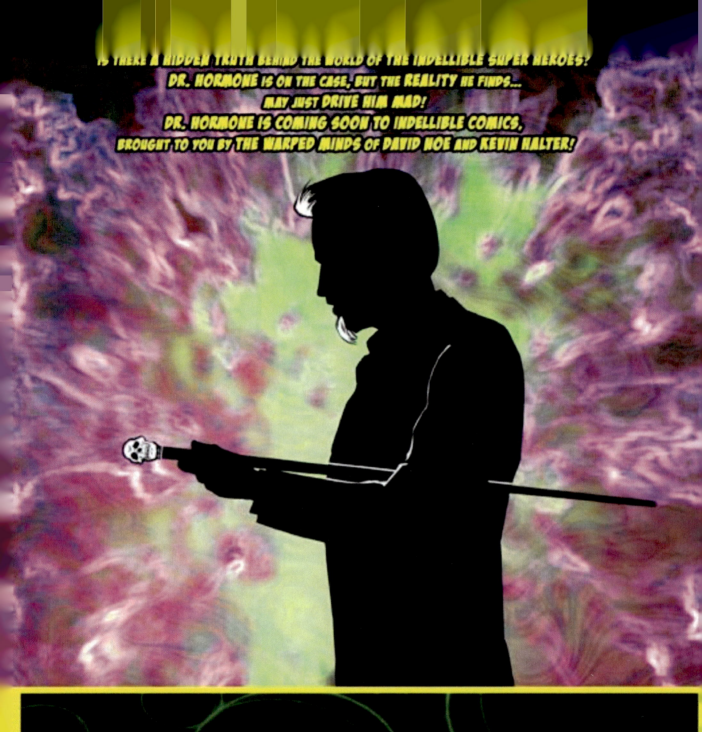

IS THERE A HIDDEN TRUTH BEHIND THE WORLD OF THE INDELLIBLE SUPER HEROES?
DR. HORMONE IS ON THE CASE, BUT THE REALITY HE FINDS...
MAY JUST DRIVE HIM MAD!
DR. HORMONE IS COMING SOON TO INDELLIBLE COMICS,
BROUGHT TO YOU BY THE WARPED MINDS OF DAVID NOE AND KEVIN HALTER!

THE AMAZING ADVENTURES OF
DR. HORMONE
BY DAVE NOE & KEVIN HALTER